Paul Foster Case

MW00641832

LEARNING TAROT ESSENTIALS

TAROT CARDS FOR BEGINNERS

Ishtar Publishing
Vancouver
www.ishtarpublishing.com

LEARNING TAROT ESSENTIALS: TAROT CARDS FOR BEGINNERS
AN ISHTAR PUBLISHING BOOK:
978-1-926667-08-9

PRINTING HISTORY
Ishtar Publishing edition published 2009

1 3 5 7 9 10 8 6 4 2

Paul Foster Case was the founder of Builders of the Adytum, a Mystery School based on the principles of Ageless Wisdom as taught in the Qabalistic-Hermetic tradition. "Adytum" is an ancient Greek word that refers to the innermost part of the Temple, the Holy of Holies, "that which is not made with hands." Builders of the Adytum is an international non-profit teaching and training Order and an outer vehicle of the Inner Spiritual Hierarchy, sometimes called the Inner School, which guides the evolution of Man.

Through Builders of the Adytum's intensely practical curriculum, which includes both lessons and rituals, students are given the opportunity to become more attuned to their innermost Reality, and so become more conscious instruments for the Life Power. They learn to turn to the Interior Teacher, whose wisdom transforms lives.

Interested readers may learn more about this organization through our website at **www.bota.org**, or by calling or writing:

Builders of the Adytum
5105 North Figueroa Street
Los Angeles, CA. 90042
Phone: 323-255-7141.

CONTENTS   PAGES

THE PATTERN ON THE TRESTLEBOARD

THIS IS TRUTH ABOUT THE SELF

0. All the power that ever was or will be is here now.

1. I am a center of expression for the primal Will-to-Good which eternally creates and sustains the universe.

2. Through me its unfailing Wisdom takes form in thought and word.

3. Filled with Understanding of its perfect law, I am guided, moment by moment, along the path of liberation.

4. From the exhaustless riches of its Limitless Substance, I draw all things needful, both spiritual and material.

5. I recognize the manifestation of the undeviating Justice in all the circumstances of my life.

6. In all things, great and small, I see the Beauty of the divine expression.

7. Living from that Will, unsupported by its unfailing Wisdom and Understanding, mine is the Victorious Life.

8. I look forward with confidence to the perfect realization of the Eternal Splendor of the Limitless Light.

9. In thought and word and deed, I rest my life, from day to day, upon the sure Foundation of Eternal Being.

10. The Kingdom of Spirit is embodied in my flesh.

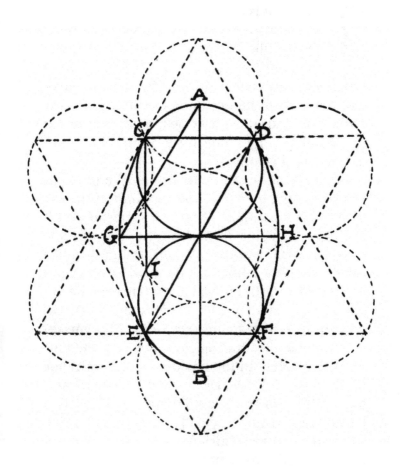

INTRODUCTION

The Tarot is a pictorial textbook of Ageless Wisdom, from whose pages have been drawn the inspiration for some of the most important works on occult science that have been published during the last seventy–five years. Its influence upon the minds of a few enlightened thinkers may be traced throughout the history of the modern revival of interest in esoteric philosophy.

This revival began in 1854 with the publication of Eliphas Levi's *Doctrine and Ritual of Transcendental Magic*, first of a series of occult writings in which he names the Tarot as his most important source of information. Eliphas Levi's teaching influenced the work of Dr. Anna Kingsford and H. P. Blavatsky; it has been developed and extended in the circles of French occultism in which *Papus* (Dr. Gerard Encausse) was so long a leading spirit; it is interpreted for English readers in the books of S. L. McGregor Mathers, A. E. Waite, Dr. W. Wynn Westcott, and others; the works of New Thought writers echo it again and again, especially the essays of Judge Thomas Troward. Curiously enough, although Levi himself was a nominal Roman Catholic, his doctrine is utilized in Scottish Rite Masonry in the United States, inasmuch as Albert Pike's Morals and Dogma of the Scottish Rite repeats verbatim page after page from the French oc cultist's *Doctrine and Ritual.*

Levi's opinion of the Tarot was very high. He says:

> As an erudite Kabalistic book, all combinations of which reveal the harmonies preexisting between signs, letters and numbers, the practical value of the Tarot is truly and above all marvelous. A prisoner devoid of books, had he only a Tarot of which he knew how to make use, could in a few years acquire a universal science, and converse with an unequalled doctrine and inexhaustible eloquence.

The aim of this analysis is to show you how to use the Tarot. A full treatment would require many volumes; but I hope to realize the promise of my title by giving a concise explanation of the general plan of the Tarot, and a brief outline of its meaning. It should be understood, however, that the student must fill in this outline with the results of his own observation and meditation.

Before entering upon the description of the construction and symbolism of this loose leaf book of occult science, it may be well to say a word as to its history. In the main, I am in agreement with A. E. Waite, who discusses the various theories as to the origin of the Tarot in his *Key to the Tarot*, published by Wm. Rider and Sons, in London. Mr. Waite concludes that the Tarot has no exoteric history before the fourteenth century. The oldest examples of Tarot designs now preserved in European museums were probably made about 1390. According to occult tradition in which I am inclined to place confidence, the real date of its invention was about the year 1200.

The inventors, this tradition avers, were a group of adepts who met at stated intervals in the city of Fez, in Morocco. After the destruction of Alexandria, Fez became the literary and scientific capital of the world. Thither, from all parts of the globe came wise men of all nations, speaking all tongues. Their conferences were made difficult by differences in language and philosophical terminology. So they hit upon the device of embodying the most important of their doctrines in a book of pictures, whose combinations should depend upon the occult harmonies of numbers. Perhaps it was a Chinese adept who suggested the idea, for the Chinese have a proverb, "One picture is worth ten thousand words," and Chinese writing is made up of conventionalized pictures. These pictures express ideas instead of words, so that the Chinese, Japanese and Koreans, if only they can write, communicate easily with each other, although they speak more than seven different languages.

As a skeleton for their invention the wise men chose the simple system of numbers and letters afforded by the Qabalah, or Secret Wisdom of Israel. Some account of that system therefore, must precede our study of the Tarot itself.

THE HEBREW WISDOM

The master key to the Hebrew wisdom is the *name* translated *Lord* in the Authorized Version of the Bible and *Jehovah* in the revised versions. It is not really a name at all, but rather a verbal, numerical and geometrical formula. In English letters corresponding to Hebrew it is spelled יהוה, I H V H. It is a form derived from the verb *to be*. Correctly translated, it means *That which was, That which is, That which shall be.* That, not *he*. Thus it is a perfect verbal symbol for the One Reality – for that Something which has always subsisted behind all forms in the eternity of the past, for that Something which really is behind all the appearances and misunderstandings of the present, for that Something which will be the foundation for all the changing forms of life expression in the eternity to come.

Never has Ageless Wisdom attempted to define this One Reality. Its inner nature defies analysis, cannot be put within the limits of any formal statement, because the One Reality is infinite. Yet the report of the wise in every age has been that in the One Something inheres the power to know. We therefore say that IHVH is a verbal symbol of the Conscious Energy that brings all things and creatures into existence.

Hebrew Wisdom classifies all possible operations of this energy into four planes, or *worlds*.

Each plane or world is represented by a letter of IHVH, as follows:

The Archetypal World. This is the world of pure ideas. In the archetypal plane are the root notions inherent in the innermost nature of the universal Conscious Energy. From these ideas are derived all the actual forms in manifestation. For example, the pure idea of a chair is the idea of sitting. And in that idea, as in all others, is embodied a volition – the will–to–sit. This will–to–sit is the single root notion behind all possible chair forms that ever have been, are now, or ever shall be. Thus the archetypal world is seen to be the plane of will–ideas. To it Ageless Wisdom assigns the element fire, representing universal radiant energy. This world and this element are represented in IHVH by the letter *I.*

The Creative World. Here the ideas of the archetypal world are specialized as particular patterns. *Sitting* becomes the mental pattern of a special kind of chair. The Cosmic Energy acting on this plane contains the patterns of all chairs that have been made or thought of in the past, of all existing in the present – but not those as yet not thought of. So with all other patterns of particular forms. To this world Ageless Wisdom assigns the element water, symbolizing the fluid plasticity of the cosmic mind stuff. The creative world is represented in IHVH by the first *H.*

The Formative World. Here the archetypal ideas, specialized in creative patterns, are brought forth into actual expression. It is the plane of processes, the world of forces behind the veil of physical things. The formative world is that which is now explored by physicists and chemists. It is the world of vibratory activities, and also the astral plane of occultism. Here take place the various kinds of action whereby the Cosmos Energy actualizes its patterns. Ageless Wisdom assigns to this world the element air, representing the life energy which wise men everywhere have associated with Breath. The formative world is represented by V in IHVH.

The Material World. This is the plane of the actual forms that affect our physical senses. Here is the process of bringing down the idea of sitting through an operation based upon the pattern of a particular chair is finally completed as the chair itself. This plane corresponds to the element earth, representing the solidity and tangibility of actual objects. It is represented by the second H in IHVH.

In each of the four worlds, Hebrew Wisdom conceives the operation of ten aspects of the universal Conscious Energy. This idea that all possible aspects of the One Reality may be reduced to a tenfold classification is found in every version of the Ageless Wisdom. Thence arises the esoteric teaching with relation to the meaning of numbers. This is a subject almost limitless in its ramifications, but what is needed for Tarot study will be found in the following paragraphs.

OCCULT MEANING OF NUMBERS

In this section we shall consider the occult significance of the numbers from Zero to Ten, with particular reference to the esoteric meanings of the so-called *Arabic* numerals. As a matter of fact, these numerals were really invented by Hindu priests, and were subsequently borrowed by the Arab mathematicians who introduced them into Europe. The key to the meaning of the numerals is the diagram accompanying this outline, now published in full for the first time. Readers of these pages who are familiar with occult symbolism will perceive that the basis of its construction is the six-pointed star, known as *The Shield of David* and *The Star of the Macrocosm.* Years ago one of the Theosophical Masters declared that the system of six circles tangent to a central seventh is a key to the construction of the cosmos, but at that time his meaning was not grasped by the student to whom the statement was made.

I hope that the inclusion of this diagram in these pages may stimulate some of my readers to further research. Want of space forbids my developing the various details here. I shall therefore content myself with saying that this one diagram is the key to the geometrical construction of the Great Pyramid, to the most accurate approximation to the squaring of the circle, to the truly occult meaning of the apron worn by Free Masons, to the correct construction of the Qabalistic diagram known as the Tree of

Life (which has been called *a key to all things*), and to the proportions of that mysterious Vault in which the body of the founder of the Rosicrucian Order is said to have been discovered. These, moreover, are but a small selection of the mysteries to which this one diagram affords a clue. But I must confine myself to its numerical significance.

In Arabic notation all numbers are represented by ten symbols, beginning with 0 and ending with 9. They are thus derived from the diagram:

0. The ellipse, representing the Cosmic Egg, whence all things come. Zero is the symbol of absence of quality, quantity, or mass. Thus it represents absolute freedom from every limitation whatsoever. It is the sign of the infinite and eternal Conscious Energy, itself No–Thing, though manifested in everything. It is That which was, is, and shall be forever, although nothing we can name. Boundless, infinitely potential, living light, it is the rootless root of all things, of all activities, of all modes of consciousness. In it are included all imaginable and unimaginable possibilities, but it transcends them all. Hebrew sages called it: (a) No–Thing; (b) The Boundless; (c) Limitless Light. Pure Conscious Energy, above and beyond thought. To us it is Superconsciousness.

The descending arc of the ellipse represents Involution, the *winding–up* process whereby Limitless Light manifests itself in name and form. At B, the lowest point of involution is reached in the mineral kingdom. B to F is the arc of *unwinding* or evolution in the inorganic world. F to H is the arc of organic development up through plants to animals. H to D is the arc of organic development from the lowest animal to the highest type of human consciousness at point D. Only a few human beings have reached this point, but the race is nearer to it now than ever before. The arc from D to A is that of conscious expression beyond human levels, the evolution of conscious oneness with the Divine. Thus the two sides of the ellipse suggest the esoteric doctrine of Involution or descent, and a corresponding Evolution, or ascent. The ascending arc corresponds to the occult doctrine: "First the stone, then the plant, then the animal, then the man, and at last the god."

1. The vertical line from A to B, connecting the extreme height with the extreme depth. The occult meanings of the number are:

Beginning, initiative, originality, unity, singleness, isolation, and the like. In Hebrew occultism it is called the Crown, to show that 1 represents the determining, ruling, directive and volitional aspect of consciousness. The Crown is also called the Primal Will. The same Hebrew philosophy calls this number the Hidden Intelligence, to show that this primary mode of consciousness is concealed behind all the veils of name and form. For this is the consciousness of the true Self or I AM, which is the Onlooker, seeing creation through countless eyes, manifesting itself through innumerable personali-

6

ties. Ageless Wisdom teaches that all things are manifestations or projections in time and space of the powers of the I AM. In short, the I AM, or number 1, is the essence, substance, energy and consciousness expressed in all forms. Everything in the universe is the self–expression of the I AM. This is the first principle, the primary existence, the First Mover. In and through human personality it manifests as the waking Self–consciousness.

2. Begins at C, follows upper circle through D to center of diagram, then through lower circle from center of diagram to E, thence horizontally from E to F. The meanings of the number are:

Duplication, reflection, receptivity, dependence, alteration, antagonism, and the like. Hebrew sages call it Wisdom, the reflection of the perfect self–consciousness of the I AM. Wisdom is the mirror wherein the I AM sees itself. The number 2 is also named Illuminating Intelligence. It is that which illuminates the personal mind. It is the aspect of universal consciousness which manifests through human personality as grasp of the inner principles of the nature of the Conscious Energy. In Hebrew occultism, 2 is also the particular number of the Life Force in all creatures. Psychologically it represents Subjective Mind.

3. Upper half same as upper part of 2, from C through D to center of diagram. Lower half from center of diagram through F and B around to E. Its meanings are:

Multiplication, development, growth, unfold-

7

ment, therefore expression. 3 signifies the actual outworking of the principles reflected from 1 by 2. In Hebrew philosophy 3 is Understanding, looking forward into the field of manifestation, in contrast to Wisdom (2), which looks back to the self-knowledge of the I AM (1). Understanding is the concrete application of abstract Wisdom. Hence it is also called Sanctifying Intelligence, to convey the idea that through growth or expression comes the perfected manifestation of the potencies latent in the Limitless Light. On the form side, perfect realization (sanctification) is perfected organism; in consciousness it is perfected faculty and function. Because all organic growth and development are thus occultly related to the number 3, this number is the symbol also of that plane of mental activity known to modern psychology as Subconsciousness.

4. Repeats vertical line of the figure 1, and adds two other lines — A to G, and G to H. Thus drawn, 4 shows in its upper portion a triangle, symbol of the number 3, and its lower portion is a T-square, symbol of 4 itself. Triangle and T-square are among the most important instruments of the draftsman. They have occult reference to the esoteric side of geometry. They suggest planning, surveying, topography and the like. From these considerations are derived the meanings of 4:

Order, measurement, classification, recording, tabulation, and so on. Because of these meanings Hebrew wisdom makes 4 the number of memory. Because the Life power's perfect memory of its own potencies and of the needs of even the least of its centers of expression cannot be supposed to fail, the idea of Beneficence (*good–givingness*) is also assigned to 4. This beneficence is not wasteful prodigality. All the gifts of the Life power are measured out. Every center of expression receives exactly what is coming to it, always. Therefore the number 4 is called the Measuring Intelligence.

5. First line horizontal, C to D; second, vertical, C to I; third, five–sixths of lower circle, from I through F and B to E. The meanings are:

Mediation (because 5 is the middle number between 1, Beginning, and 9, Completion), adaptation, means, agency, activity, process, and the like. 5 is the dynamic Law proceeding from abstract Order (4).

To primitive minds, the working of Law seems to be the operation of many forces, mostly hostile to man. Hence 5 is the number of versatility, and one of its names in Hebrew occultism is Fear. Ignorant people endeavor to propitiate the power they fear. Their sacrifices are the beginning of religious ritual.   Hence 5 is the number of religion.

A better, though incomplete, knowledge of Law sees it as a relentless, harsh, mechanical expression of mathematical principles, taking no account of human needs or aspirations. This is the interpretation of the materialist, who sees the Law as a mighty power. Hebrew sages take account of this also, and say that 5 is the number of Strength and Severity, as well as of Fear.

Finally, to seers and sages, Law appears as the manifestation of perfect Justice, whereby man, whose numeral symbol is also 5, may so adapt natural conditions that he may realize progressive liberation from every kind of bondage.

5, then, is the number of versatility, because it shows the changing aspects of the One Law, inspiring fear in the ignorant, perceived by the materialist as relentless strength, and understood by the wise as undeviating justice. This One Law is the root of all operations of the Life power, and is therefore called Radical Intelligence. The root consciousness expressed through human personality in this One Law of mediation or adaptation. Man can change conditions. This is the secret of his power to realize freedom.

6. A continuous line from D to A, down through the ellipse (on the Involution curve) to B, then around the lower circle to B. Its symmetry suggests the philosophical conception of Beauty. This is the direct outcome of ideas represented by the preceding numerals. A free Life power (0), knowing itself perfectly (1), grasping all the possibilities of what it is in itself (2), understanding just how to work those possibilities out into expression (3), never forgetting itself, or any detail of the perfect order of its self–manifestation (4), and developing that order through the agency of a perfectly just law or method (5), must inevitably be working toward a perfectly symmetrical, balanced, and therefore beauti-

ful, result. This idea is implicit in the following meanings of 6:

Balance, equilibration, symmetry, beauty; harmony of opposites, reciprocity; complementary activities, polarity, love. It is named Intelligence of Mediating Influence, or Intelligence of the Separated Emanations.

7. Horizontal line, C to D; diagonal line, D to E. To exhaust the meanings of this number would take as many pages as an encyclopedia. It is the great Biblical number, many books in both Old and New Testaments being written on a plan of sevens – seven chapters, seven subdivisions, and so on. On this point see the literary introductions in Moulton's Modern Readers' Bible. The more important occult meanings are:

Rest, safety, security, victory. 7 represented temporary cessation to the ancients, not final perfection, as some have thought. In Hebrew the word for *seven* and that for *oath* are closely related, since the security and safety of a sworn compact were represented in the Hebrew mind by 7.

This number stands for the logical consequence of the preceding ideas. A perfect Life power, working in the way outlined in the explanation of 6, cannot be supposed to fail. Omnipotence must ultimately, no matter what present appearances may be, arrive at a triumphantly successful conclusion in its undertakings. The Great Work is as yet unfinished. The Cosmic Experiment has not come to completion; but when we consider the nature of the Source of that experiment, the nature of the Worker in that work, reason assures us that it must succeed, down to the minutest detail. The Hebrew name of 7 is Occult Intelligence.

8 is composed of the upper and lower circles within the ellipse. In writing it we begin at A, describe a descending "S" to B, and return on an ascending inverted "S" to A. Thus the form of the figure suggests vibration by the shape of the lines, and alternation by the two kinds of motion. It is also the only figure except 0 which may be written over and over again without lifting pen from paper. Thus in mathematics the figure 8 written horizontally is the sign of infinity. Its occult meanings are:

Rhythm, alternate cycles or involution and evolution, vibration, flux and reflux, and the like. It also represents the fact that opposite forms of expression (that is, all pairs of opposites) are effects of a single Cause. (See on this point, Isaiah 45, verses 5 to 7). This number 8 is the digit value of the name IHVH (Jehovah), 888 is the numeration of the name Jesus in Greek, and 8 is not only the *Dominical Number*, or *Number of the Lord*, but is also the particular number of the *god* called Thoth by Egyptians, Nebo by Assyrians, Hermes by Greeks, and Mercury by Romans. Thus 8 is preeminently the number of magic and Hermetic Science. Its Hebrew name is Splendor, and the aspect of consciousness to which it corresponds is called Perfect Intelligence. The Hebrew word translated *perfect* is שלם, ShLM, rendered in English as *Salem*. It also signifies *peace.*

9. Begins at D, follows upper circle down to center of diagram, continues back to D, then along line of ellipse to E. As last of the numeral symbols 9 represents the following ideas:

Completion, attainment, realization, the goal of endeavor, the end of a cycle of activity. But because 8 indicates Rhythm as part of the creative process, completion is not absolute cessation. The end of one cycle is the beginning of another. This fact is the basis of all practical occultism. Nobody ever comes to the end of his tether. Nobody ever reaches a point where nothing more remains to be hoped for, where nothing is left to be accomplished. Every End is the seed of a fresh Beginning. In Hebrew wisdom, therefore, 9 is called Basis or Foundation, and corresponds to the mode of consciousness called Pure or Clear Intelligence, because the completion of any process is the pure, clear, unadulterated expression of the intention or idea which initiated that process.

10. Combines the ellipse of superconsciousness (0), with the vertical line of self–consciousness (1). It is the number of perfection, of dominion, of realization. Read from right to left, from units to tens (as all figures should be read symbolically) it suggests the outpouring of the limitless Life power through the initiative, specialization and concentration of the I AM. In Hebrew occultism the number 10 is called Kingdom, and the mode of consciousness assigned to it is Resplendent Intelligence, – that

is, brilliant, glowing, full of life and power. This mode of intelligence is said in one esoteric text to have its seat in Understanding, and Understanding is the number 3, or Sanctifying Intelligence. What is meant is that in order to have the resplendent, glorious consciousness of mastery, one must have also as a basis the sanctifying, perfecting organizing power of Understanding. Our citizenship in the Kingdom of Heaven on Earth is determined by the degree of our understanding.

Such is the outline of the meaning of the ten primary numbers according to the Ageless Wisdom, as handed down to us through the Sages of Israel. It is the basic clue to the meaning of the Tarot. For instance, the whole book contains 78 pages. Interpreting the number 78 from the foregoing, we see that it is the number representing the expression of the Splendor of the Perfect Intelligence (8) through the Victory of Occult Intelligence (7). Precisely this is the general purpose of the Tarot as a whole.

CONSTRUCTION OF THE TAROT

The Tarot is a book disguised as a pack of cards. Fifty–six of its seventy–eight pages are called minor trumps. These are divided into four suits corresponding to the four worlds previously explained. The wands (clubs) correspond to the archetypal world, the element fire, and I in IHVH; the cups (hearts) correspond to the creative world, the element water, and the first H in IHVH; the swords (spades) correspond to the formative world, the element air, and the V in IHVH; the pentacles or coins (diamonds) correspond to the material world, the element earth, and the second H in IHVH.

In each suit are ten minor trumps numbered consecutively from Ace (One) to Ten. Thus the meaning of any numbered card in the minor trumps may be determined by combining the meanings of its number with the characteristics of the world represented by its suit. All the Twos, for example, suggest duplication, alternation, and the like, and all of them convey some suggestion of Wisdom. So with the other numbered cards.

Besides the numbered cards, each suit of minor trumps contains four court cards, instead of the three found in modern packs of playing–cards. They are:

KING: symbol of spirit, or essential Self in man

QUEEN: symbol of soul, the inner *pattern* part of a particular man

KNIGHT: symbol of personal energies, or the special processes peculiar to a particular human being

PAGE: symbol of body, or external vehicle of a particular person.

The King of Wands is the idea of spirit, the Queen of Wands the idea of soul, the Knight of Wands the idea of personal energies, the Page of Wands the idea of body. Similarly the court–cards of Cups present the patterns of spirit, soul, personal energies and body; those of Swords represent the processes in manifesting spirit, soul, personal energies and body; those of Pentacles represent the actualized manifestation of spirit, soul, personal energies and body.

The more important part of the Tarot consists of the twenty–two cards called major trumps. These are pictures, numbered consecutively from Zero to Twenty–one. Every major trump has a special title, which affords an important clue to its meaning. In addition, every major trump represents one of the twenty–two letters of the Hebrew alphabet.

This alphabet differs from others in that every letter has a name. Thus the twenty–two letter names describe twenty–two natural objects. They follow each other in logical sequence, bringing to the mind's eye a series of pictures. These pictures call up in every human mind, irrespective of race, certain basic associations of ideas. Thus in studying any major trump of the Tarot we begin with the mental image called up by the name of the Hebrew letter to which it corresponds.

In addition to the clues afforded by the numbers, titles and letter names are others derived from occult meanings of the letters given in a very ancient volume of Hebrew wisdom–teaching. The name of this book is the *Sepher Yetzirah*, or *Book of Formation*. From this book are taken all the occult attributions of the Hebrew alphabet given herein, with the exception of the attributions of the Sun, Moon and planets to the double letters.

These planetary attributions to the double letters are purposely mixed in all the ancient copies of the *Book of Formation*, in order to mislead uninitiated readers into whose hands the book might fall. The correct attributions were reserved for mouth–to–ear instruction. They have never appeared in print outside works written by me, except in one article published in the *Occult Review* for March, 1910, and in certain other writings given out or more or less directly inspired by the author of that article. He received the information from an occult society, under seals of secrecy which were violated by his publication of the true correspondence. I worked out the correct arrangement from certain hints given in the Book of Formation, and from the Tarot itself, in the year 1907. My knowledge of the attributions was therefore in the nature of a recovery, and I am not under obligation to keep it secret.

Instead of tabulating all the letters and their meanings together, I shall make a separate explanation of each letter in connection with the major trump to which it corresponds. The various meanings and attributions should be read, digested and elaborated by every student who seeks to arrive at the deeper significance of the Tarot.

It remains only to be said that the following descriptions of the symbolism are in the main based upon the most recent edition of the Tarot, that known as the "Rider pack," drawn by Miss Pamela Coleman Smith under the supervision of Mr. A. E. Waite. Mr. Waite has had access to many occult manuscripts relating to the Tarot, and although he has recently shown an unaccountable disposition to throw dust in the eyes of the uninitiated by pretending to believe that the attribution of the cards to the letters used in these pages is not the correct arrangement, his own rectifications of the symbolism and numbering of the earlier exoteric versions of this picture book of Ageless Wisdom are evidence enough that he really understands the validity of this attribution. For example, in accordance with an old esoteric tradition, he has transposed the numbering of the cards named Strength and Justice. In exoteric editions of the Tarot current in Italy and France subsequent to the eighteenth century, Strength was numbered XI, and Justice was numbered VIII. In the Rider pack these numbers are reversed, as they are in Tarot packs belonging to certain occult schools. The reason is that whatever card is numbered VIII represents the zodiacal sign Leo, and the picture entitled Strength shows a woman taming a red lion. Similarly, whatever card is numbered XI corresponds to the sign Libra, and the picture entitled Justice shows a woman carrying the scales (Libra). Furthermore, there are many little details in some of the pictures which depend for their meaning upon this same attribution of the major trumps to the Hebrew letters. I shall point these out as we come to them.

THE ATTRIBUTION OF THE MAJOR TRUMPS TO THE HEBREW ALPHABET

This is the crux in Tarot study. As I have said, the true arrangement has never been printed except in books of my own, and in works traceable to the influence of a writer who betrayed an obligation to secrecy in publishing it. Eliphas Levi knew it, but could not give it, since he also received it in a secret order. He did, however, announce the fact that the major trumps correspond to the Hebrew alphabet; and then proceeded to give an attribution whose very absurdity should have warned his readers that it is incorrect.

The absurdity consists in putting the picture numbered Zero between those numbered Twenty and Twenty-one. But Eliphas Levi deliberately chose this position for the Zero card, because it was then assigned to the only letter in the Hebrew alphabet (besides the one to which it rightly belongs) that is a symbol of Spirit. For the letter Shin, next to the last in the Hebrew alphabet, has the value of 300, and 300 is the numeration of the Hebrew words אלהים רוח, RVCh ALHIM, Ruach Elohim. The English of these words is Life Breath of the gods, or Spirit of God. Hence Shin, by Hebrew wise men, is called the *Holy Letter*, because its number is the number of the name of the Divine

Spirit. There is, however, another letter in the alphabet which is also a symbol of Spirit, or Life Breath, and this is Aleph, the first letter.

By attributing the Zero trump to this letter we put it in its true place in the series of major trumps. For in a series of numbered pictures including Zero and ending with Twenty–one, the logical place for Zero is at the beginning of the series, because Zero represents the No–Thing which we must think of as subsisting before the manifestation of the relative Unity or beginning represented by 1.

Arranging the major trumps in this order, then, the complete attribution to the letters of the Hebrew alphabet is as follows:

O.   The Fool, א, Aleph
I.   The Magician, ב, Beth
II.   The High Priestess, ג, Gimel
III.   The Empress, ד, Daleth
IV.   The Emperor, ה, Heh
V.   The Hierophant, ו, Vau
VI.   The Lover, ז, Zain
VII.   The Chariot, ח, Cheth
VIII.   Strength, ט, Teth
IX.   The Hermit, י, Yod
X.   The Wheel of Fortune, כ, Kaph
XI.   Justice, ל, Lamed
XII.   The Hanged Man, מ, Mem
XIII.   Death, נ, Nun
XIV.   Temperance, ס, Samekh
XV.   The Devil, ע, Ayin
XVI.   The Tower, פ, Peh

XVII.   The Star, **צ**, Tzaddi
XVIII. The Moon, **ק**, Qoph
XIX.   The Sun, **ר**, Resh
XX.   The Judgment, **ש**, Shin
XXI.   The World, **ת**, Tau

Readers who may be familiar with the fact that Hebrew letters have numeral values need not be confused by this arrangement, although it does make the trump numbered I correspond to Beth, the letter whose value is 2. The numerals on the major trumps run in serial order. The numbers of the letters, on the contrary, are not in series. From Aleph to Teth the letter values are the digits from 1 to 9; from Yod to Tzaddi they are reckoned in tens, from 10 to 90; and the last four letters have the values, 100, 200, 300 and 400 respectively. As a matter of fact the letter values are used in occultism chiefly for determining the numeration of words. They do not have the occult significance that attaches to the numbers printed on the major trumps. The latter, moreover, are serial numbers establishing the order of the Tarot pictures.

In connection with the following explanations, you will find it useful to arrange the major trumps on a table in the following order.

O

I	II	III	IV	V	VI	VII
VIII	IX	X	XI	XII	XIII	XIV
XV	XVI	XVII	XVIII	XIX	XX	XXI

In this arrangement the Zero card is placed above the others to indicate that it precedes the whole series, and is not really in the sequence of numbers. The pictures in the top row refer to powers or potencies; those in the middle row are symbols of laws or agencies; those in the bottom row represent conditions or effects. Thus II is the power which works through the agency of VIII to modify the conditions or effects represented by XV; I is the power which works through the agency of IX to modify the conditions represented by XVI, and so on through the series.

We may now proceed to the explanation of the separate pictures of the major trumps.

THE FOOL

Aleph, **א**, is the Hebrew equivalent of English A and has the numeral value 1. Its name means Bull or Ox. This establishes the time of the invention of this alphabet as being during the astronomical period called the Taurean Age, when the Bull was the god–symbol dominant in the religions of the ancient world. Apis in Egypt, Mithra among the Persians, Dionysus among the Greeks all had the bull or ox as a symbol. Since oxen pulled the plow and threshed the grain in primitive husbandry, they became symbols of the motive power in agriculture. Agriculture is the basic form of civilization, thus the ox is the representative of the power at work in all forms of human adaptation and modification of natural conditions. Oxen and bulls, the world over, are symbols of creative energy, Life power, the vital principle of plants, animals and men, which comes to us in physical form as the energy of the sun.

Ruach, literally *Breath*, is the Hebrew name for this vital principle. It is equivalent to English *Spirit*, Latin *Spiritus*, Greek *Pneuma*, and Sanskrit *Prana* – all meaning literally air or breath, and secondarily, the all–pervading cosmic life energy animating every living creature.

Fiery or Scintillating Intelligence is the mode of consciousness represented by Aleph. Breath keeps a fire going in our bodies. In both Old and

New Testaments we are told: "The Lord our God is a consuming fire." To define the primal mode of the Life power – the first aspect of the cosmic vital principle – is impossible. Yet wise men have ever agreed that it is like fire, and the most recent discoveries of physics likewise show that the fundamental *something* whereof all things are made is a radiant, fiery energy. Occultism adds the thought that this energy is the working power of pure consciousness, which plays upon that energy, is inseparable from it, and directs all its manifestations from within. This idea of inherent directing consciousness, combined with the current scientific explanations of the electromagnetic constitution of matters gives precisely the conception which Hebrew sages convey in the term Scintillating Intelligence.

In the color scale used in Western schools of occult science, the element Air and the Fiery Life Breath are represented by a pale, clear shade of yellow. Since the discovery of the planet Uranus, the higher octave of Mercury, this planet has been attributed to Aleph, and is represented by the yellow tint just mentioned. Its tone vibration is E–natural. The name Uranus, it should be noted, is the English adaptation of the Greek word meaning *sky*.

The Zero trump represents all the foregoing ideas. Its number identifies it with that No–Thing whence all things proceed, which Hebrew sages called Limitless Light. In connection with the letter Aleph, however, we find that Light represented as the active principle of existence, before actual manifestation. The picture, therefore, does not show that principle as it really is, because the Absolute transcends finite comprehension. The symbols show it as it has revealed itself, in a measure, to the wise.

The Fool is shown as a youth, because we must think of the Absolute in terms of our own experience. To our minds the Life Breath presents itself in human form; but behind this personal seeming, sages discern something higher, typified in the picture by the white sun. That higher something is an impersonal power, manifesting as the limitless energy radiated to the planets of world systems without number, streaming to them from their respective suns.

In manifestation, this energy is temporarily limited by living organisms. Of these the primary class is the vegetable kingdom, represented by the green wreath which binds the Fool's fair hair. The hair itself is yellow, symbolizing the radiant energy of the Life Breath. The higher class of organisms is the animal kingdom, evolved from the vegetable world, and represented by the red feather rising from the wreath. This feather is also a symbol of aspiration and of truth. The colors of wreath and feather, green and red, are complimentary, as are the kingdoms they symbolize.

The cosmic Life Breath is forever young, forever in the morning of its power, forever on the verge of the abyss of manifestation. It always faces unknown possibilities of self–expression transcending any height it may have reached at a given time. On this account the sun behind the traveler is at an angle of forty–five degrees in the eastern heaven, as Swedenborg says the celestial sun remains forever in the spiritual world. The sun never reaches the zenith, for from the zenith it would have to descend, and the idea here intended is that infinite energy never can reach a point in manifestation whence it must begin to decrease in power. On this account, too, the Fool faces West, toward the direction that represents in symbolism the unknown. His eager gaze is fixed rapturously upon a distant height beyond and above him. He is That which was, and is, and shall be – the deathless, fadeless life principle subsisting eternally behind all modes of existence.

His inner robe is dazzling white, representing the light of perfect wisdom. It is almost wholly concealed by the black coat of ignorance, lined with the red of passion, fire, and material force. This outer garment is embroidered with what seems to be a floral decoration, but the unit of design (repeated ten times) is a yellow wheel, containing eight red spokes. Around this wheel are seven green trefoils. The yellow color of the wheel represent air or breath; the eight red spokes combine the number 8, symbol of rhythm, with the color red, and refer to the rhythmic action of the fiery activity which sets the Life Breath into wheeling, whirling motion. The seven trefoils are green, color of organic life in the vegetable kingdom, and particular color of the planet Venus in color symbolism. Each represents one of the *seven Spirits of God*, or seven creative forces. They are trefoils because every one of these seven forces has a triple expression: (a) integrating, (b) equilibrating, and (c) disintegrating. There are ten repetitions of this unit of design, to refer to the ancient doctrine that all manifestation is in ten aspects or phases: "Ten ineffable numerations, ten and not nine, ten and not eleven," – as the *Book of Formation* says. In addition to these ten wheels, there is on the right breast of the Fool a formless yellow ornament enclosing a triple tongue of red. This represents the state of the Life Breath prior to manifestation, when the universal energy (yellow) although it has the triple potency of expression (the triple red flame) within itself, has not yet organized that potency into the rhythmic whirling motion which is the basis of all modes of expression.

The black wand over the Fool's right shoulder is a measuring tool. It is a symbol of will, of which attention (the wand itself) is the essence, and to which memory (the wallet) is closely linked. The wallet contains the summed up experience of previous manifestations because at the beginning of every new cycle of self–expression the Life power carries with it the essence of all its experiences in former cycles. The wallet has a dim representation of an eagle's head. This refers to the zodiacal sign Scorpio, and is an intimation that the wand and wallet together may be understood as phallic emblems, referring to the natural process whereby the accumulated experience of the Life power is passed on from cycle to cycle, through an endless chain of living organisms.

The rose in the Fool's left hand is white, to indicate freedom from desire and passion, and also to show that it refers to the spiritual proto-type of desire. It is a cultivated flower, showing (as do other details of the traveler's vestments and equipment) that he has come from a pre-vious scene of cultural activity, from a plain somewhere behind him on his journey. For as corresponding to Aleph, the Fool symbolizes cultural activities. The leaves of the rose must be some multiple of 5 (adaptation) and the six leaves on the stem are to be understood as rep-resenting ideas associated with the number 6. Note that the leaves are disposed in a balanced symmetry, three on either side of the stem.

At the waist the black robe is encircled by a gir-dle having twelve circular ornaments, of which seven are visible. It refers to the twelve signs of the zodiac, through which are expressed the powers of the seven heavenly bodies known to the ancient world. Thus the girdle typifies Time, and since the belt must be removed in order to take off the black robe, here is a plain intima-tion that to rid ourselves of ignorance and pas-sion we must overcome the illusion of Time, which is, as Kant long since proved, purely a creation of the human intellect. The practical occultist learns to substitute Eternity for Time, and practices daily to accustom himself to lead-ing the timeless life.

The citrine or olive of the Fool's hose (the tint varies in various versions of the Tarot) refers to the element of earth, and to the tenth *numeration*, the Kingdom. His yellow shoes refer to the element of air, which is the vehicle of the Life power.

The icy peaks in the distance show that the cold, abstract principles of mathematics are above and behind all the warm, colorful, vital activities of cosmic manifestation.

The little white dog is a descendant of wolves and jackals. Thus he is a human adaptation, whereby something given in a wild and dangerous state by the unmodified processes of nature, has been changed into a friend, helper, and companion of man. He also indicates the truth that all subhuman forms of the Life power are elevated and improved by the advance of human consciousness. Finally, for symbolic reasons going back to ancient Egypt, he is a symbol of intellect, subordinate to superconsciousness.

The Fool, then, symbolizes what Mr. Waite, who supervised the design of this version, calls "the state of the first emanation." He is the primary aspect of universal consciousness, which we term Superconsciousness. He is the cosmic Life Breath, about to descend into the abyss of manifestation. Because he symbolizes the state of the Life power just prior to beginning a cycle of self-expression, he also represents inexperience. For until the Life power actually enters into the particular activities of such a cycle, it can have no real experience of those activities.

It is because of this inexperience that the subtle wise men who invented the Tarot called this trump *The Fool*. Another reason was that they were familiar with the philosophic truth that superconsciousness is above reason, imagination, thought, feeling, and all other states of self–consciousness. *The Mystical Theology of Dionysus* therefore says of God: "He has neither imagination nor reason, nor does He know anything as it is, nor does anything know Him as He is." Apply these words to a man and you call him a fool. Furthermore, the attempt to limit Divine Consciousness to personality, making God a big man, is mentally to create a foolish divinity. Finally, the title of the Zero card refers to that "foolishness of God, which is wiser than men." This means that although superconsciousness has no actual experience of those facts and events which are the warp and woof of human knowledge, its inherent knowledge of the principles of its own nature far transcends the lesser knowledge of human wisdom.

THE MAGICIAN

B eth (ב, B, value 2), means *house.* The first thing about a house is its location, determined by survey, an application of geometry. In its building architecture, geometry, adaptation of materials, and many other practical applications of science are involved. Time was when the whole art of building was called a *mystery,* and was under the direction of the priests of Thoth–Nebo–Hermes–Mercury. House–building is part of Hermetic science, and survivals of this idea are preserved in the rituals of Free Masonry.

Mercury is the astrological attribution to Beth. It represents both the planet and the *god.* Understand by *god* an aspect of universal consciousness personified. The *gods* are the Elohim of the Hebrew Scriptures, wherein it is written of man, "I said, Ye are gods." To Mercury or Hermes (Hiram) the Egyptians attributed their forty–two books of science, embracing astronomy, astrology, arithmetic, geometry, medicine, grammar, logic, rhetoric, music, magic, and so on. Mercury or Hermes was the great magician and transformer, bearing the caduceus, or wand of miracles, which survives to this day as a symbol of the healing art. Nevertheless, he was only the messenger of a divinity higher than himself – merely the transmitter, not the originator, the channel rather than the source.

Astrologically, the Mercury vibration represents intellect. In the color scale used throughout these lessons it is yellow, color of Air, but a deeper tint than that assigned to Uranus. The musical tone is the same, E–natural.

Beth is one of the seven double letters, so called because they have in Hebrew both a hard and a soft pronunciation. To every double letter is assigned a pair of opposites. To Mercury and Beth, because the planet and letter designate an aspect of consciousness which destroys as easily as it constructs, the pair assigned is life and death.

Intelligence of Transparency is the mode of consciousness. *Transparency* means *letting light shine through.* Here we have the same idea of transmission that is suggested by Hermes as transmitter of the messages of the higher divinity. Clearly, the mode of consciousness called transparent must be one which affords a free channel of communication, which permits the free passage downward and outward of the super conscious Light which is both above and within.

Above is the direction assigned to Beth, because the mode of consciousness corresponding to the letter is the superior term of human personal consciousness. As Hermes was heralded of the gods, directing the soul (according to Egyptian mythology) through the mysteries of the underworld or night side of nature, so this superior phase of human personal consciousness is the initiator, the conductor of personality through the mazes of life. It is the number ONE consciousness, the Ego–consciousness, the *I am I*, which modern psychologists sometimes call *objective mind*, but which I prefer to term self–consciousness. It is the Onlooker, the director, the superior personal mode of universal Conscious Energy. It is your everyday waking consciousness.

The Magician is the correct title, used in all versions of the Tarot belonging to occult fraternities, although it is sometimes debased into *Juggler* in the exoteric packs. Magic is simply the ancient name for science, particularly for Hermetic science. The true magic presides over house–building, because it shows us how to erect actual houses so as to take advantage of the occult properties of the earth currents of magnetic vibration. It presides over life and death because it has to do with laws and principles whereby self–conscious states of mind initiate and determine subconscious reactions. Those reactions are for life or death, according to the patterns which the self–conscious mind formulates and passes down to the subconscious plane. Every true magician, moreover, knows that all his practice has a mathematical and geometrical basis. By the aid of occult geometry he has traced nature to her concealed recesses, and uses geometrical diagrams and formulae in his practical work. Finally, though he knows himself to be above nature, he also understands that his operations succeed to the degree that his thought, word and action faithfully transmit the forces of the plane above him. The greatest magicians know themselves to be no more than channels of the Life power, clear window panes through which the light of wisdom within the house of personality streams forth into the objective world.

The arbor of roses over his head corresponds to the letter name, Beth, because an arbor is the simplest type of house. Red roses, symbols of Venus, represent the desire nature. Here they suggest that the power which the Magician draws from above is modified or qualified by desire. This is true of all self–conscious activity. Every moment of our waking consciousness is motivated and conditioned by some type of desire.

The horizontal figure 8 over the Magician's head is the ancient occult number ascribed to Hermes. (See explanation of the number 8.) It is also an ancient sign of the Holy Spirit. Placed horizontally it means dominion on the horizontal plane, that is, dominion in material affairs, because the horizontal line is one of the oldest symbols of matter.

In contrast to the Fool's yellow locks, the black hair of the Magician signifies ignorance, but ignorance limited by knowledge. For a white crown encircles the Magus' brow and it passes around his forehead at the location of the brain areas particularly active in self–conscious mentation.

The uplifted right hand suggests power drawn from above. The wand it holds aloft is a double–ended phallic symbol. It is phallic, because the nerve force used to maintain the reproductive functions may be purified and sublimated by certain magical exercises. The purification is suggested by the whiteness of the wand. The two points, exactly alike in form, remind us of the Hermetic axiom, "That which is below is as that which is above, and that which is above is as that which is below, for the performance of the miracles of the One Thing." They also indicate subtly that the lower manifestations of the force here symbolized are not destroyed or atrophied in the process of purification and sublimation. Finally, the two points refer to the duality of magical operations which are of two great classes – those leading to life, and those resulting in death.

The down–pointing left hand symbolizes direction of power to a plane below. It makes the gesture of concentration. The pointing finger is that attributed to the planet Jupiter. From this finger palmists determine the degree of a client's powers of leadership and direction. It is the executive and determinative finger. The gesture plainly conveys the notion that concentration is the secret of the direction and control of forces below the plane of self–conscious awareness.

Of the double gesture made by the Magician's hands Mr. Waite says: "This dual sign is known in very high grades of the Instituted Mysteries; it shows the descent of grace, virtue and light, drawn from things above and derived to things below. The suggestion throughout is therefore the possession and communication of the Powers and Gifts of the Spirit."

The white inner robe of the Magician has the same significance as the white garment of the Fool. The serpent girdle signifies wisdom (serpent) and eternity (biting his tail). Mr. Waite says that "here it indicates more especially the eternity of attainment in the spirit." Thus it is colored blue, showing eternal wisdom manifested in substance, for blue is the color of water, the element which particularly refers to the plastic mind stuff of the creative world. The red outer garment represents desire, passion and activity. Its color is that of the planet Mars, which astrology associates with action and initiative. The red robe has no binding girdle. It may be slipped on or off at will. This means that self–consciousness may enter into action or abstain from it, according to circumstances. This intimates the power of choice, or of selection, characteristic of self–consciousness.

The table before the Magician represents the *field of attention* in modern psychology. The word *table* also has affinities in language with the word *measurement*, inasmuch as to classify and arrange is to tabulate. Note that the corners of the table had to be squared, and that the cylindrical legs, which have capitals like pillars, required the use of compasses and suggest the *orders* of architecture.

"On the table in front of the Magician," says Mr. Waite, "are the implements of the four Tarot suits, signifying the elements of natural life, which lie like counters before the adept, and he

36

adapts them as he wills." As elements of natural life they refer to fire (wand), water (cup), air (sword) and earth (pentacle). They also symbolize the four worlds and the letters of IHVH. The Magician's problem is to arrange them in proper order. In ceremonial magic these implements are the staff, the cup of libations and divination, the magic sword, and the pentacle. On the pentacle are written or engraved geometrical figures, words, numbers and sigils in accordance with the nature of the work. In this instance the sigil on the pentacle is the Pentagram, pentalpha, or five–pointed star. Of this sign Eliphas Levi says:

> The Pentagram expresses the mind's domination over the elements and it is by this sign that we bind the demons of the air, the spirits of fire, the spectres of water, and the ghosts of earth. It is the star of the Magi, the burning star of the Gnostic schools, the sign of intellectual omnipotence and autocracy. It is the symbol of the Word made Flesh.
> . . The sign of the Pentagram is called also the sign of the Microcosm. Its complete comprehension is the key of the two worlds – it is absolute natural philosophy and natural science.

From the foregoing quotation you may come to understand the nature of the work to which the Magician in this picture is dedicating his powers. Be careful not to take the first sentence of the quotation too literally. There is a meaning behind the surface meaning. Find it yourself.

In practical everyday life the implements of the Magician are the four life essentials: light (wand), water (cup), air (sword) and food (pentacle). The combination of these life essentials in proper order and proportions is the task of every practical occultist.

Finally, the four implements correspond to four ancient esoteric admonitions, which sum up the whole practical application of occult law. These admonitions are: (1) TO WILL (wand); (2) TO KNOW (cup); (3) TO DARE (sword); (4) TO BE SILENT (pentacle). The last, in some respects, is the most important. *Occult* means *hidden*, and one of the first duties of a practical occultist is the practice of silence.

The garden is the antithesis to the barren height whereon stands the Fool. It is fertile and productive. It represents the subjective and subconscious planes of mental activity. The subjective may be compared to the surface, or outer crust, of the ground. The subconsciousness is the teeming soil beneath. The Magician is here shown as a gardener, like Adam, of whom an old legend says that he was put in the Garden of Eden to grow roses. Like Adam, self–consciousness is the namer of objects. Like Adam, personal self–consciousness is formed by the power of the *Lord*, who is That which was, is and shall be. Like Adam, too, it is formed of the *dust of the ground*, because self–consciousness is an aggregate of innumerable tiny sense impressions (dust) originating in that cosmic operation of the Life power which makes the environment of personality, and is the true ground or basis of all self–conscious experience.

"Beneath," writes Mr. Waite, "are roses and lilies, the flos campi and lilium convallium, changed into garden flowers, to show the culture of aspiration." Red roses typify Venus and the desire nature. White lilies represent abstract thought, untinged by desire. Roses are developed from the five petalled wild rose, and thus symbolize the number 5, whose geometrical correspondence is the Pentagram. As symbols of desire, they represent that phase of subconscious response to self–conscious direction that has to do with art, invention, and the adaptation of the principles of abstract truth to practical ends. Lilies have six petals, and in cross section their flowers show the Hexagram, or six–pointed star, which is the symbol of the Macrocosm. Pure science concerns itself with the laws of the Macrocosm, apart from their use by human inventions.

Thus all the meanings of the letter, the number and the picture show us the powers of the self–conscious phase of mental activity. Those powers are primarily directed to the control of forces and things below the self–conscious level. The energy utilized comes from above, from superconsciousness. It is fixed and modified by acts of attention. Concentration is the great secret of the magical art. True concentration is perfect transparency, in which personality becomes the free, unobstructed channel for the super conscious radiant energy. Herein is the secret of true volition, and Eliphas Levi tells us, "All magic is in the will."

THE HIGH PRIESTESS

Gimel, ג, third letter of the Hebrew alphabet, is a double letter. Its name means *camel*. Because camels are used for transportation, for carrying goods from one place to another, it signifies travel, communication, commerce, and like ideas. Because merchants and pilgrims use camels for making journeys together, it suggests combination, association, coexistence, partnership, and the like. Because a camel has means of carrying extra supplies of water, it symbolizes moisture. Finally, it is the *ship of the desert*, and its humps look somewhat like the horns of a crescent.

Gimel is represented in English by the letter *G*. Its numeral value in Hebrew arithmetic, and in reckoning the values of Hebrew words, is 3.

The Moon is the celestial body assigned to Gimel. First, because the Moon is a satellite, accompanying the earth. Second, because the Moon waxes and wanes, just as a caravan is first seen as a tiny dust cloud on the rim of the desert, then grows larger and larger until it stops for awhile at some oasis city, and then grows smaller and smaller as it journeys thence on its way to its next destination. Third, because the lunar crescent resembles the shape of the camel's humps, also because the Moon is the *ship of the skies*. Finally, the astrological nature of the Moon is cold and moist. The Moon is the astrological symbol of personality, and particularly of the memories carried from incarnation to incarnation by the subjective mind. Its color is blue, its musical tone G–sharp or A–flat.

As a double letter, Gimel designates the pair of opposites, peace and strife. For, as in the world peace and war are mainly dictated by the conditions of commerce, communication and transportation, so, in human personality, adjustment or maladjustment are largely determined by the response of the subjective mind to the things and people with whom we are brought into communication.

Uniting Intelligence is the type of consciousness attributed to Gimel. As transportation (camel and caravan) brings distant places nearer together, and establishes communication between them, so does the subjective mind, which is the connecting medium between human personalities unite us to each other – regardless of distance, because the subjective mind is the vehicle of telepathic communication.

Below is the direction attributed to Gimel. That which is below is secondary, subordinate, dependent, under control, subject to command, obedient. All these ideas are clearly related to the idea of *camel* as the obedient beast of burden. They relate in consciousness to the subordinate element of personal consciousness, the subjective mind, which is at all times amenable to control by suggestions originating in self–consciousness.

High Priestess means literally *chief feminine*

elder, or primary receptive aspect of the Life power. In Hindu philosophy this is Prakriti, the precosmic root substance which is the substratum beneath all the objective planes of existence. Thus she is identical in one sense with the First Mother, or First Matter, of the alchemists, who often call the First Matter their Virgin Diana. Diana is the goddess of the crescent Moon. She is also the Great Hecate of Greek occult philosophy. Hecate, often confused in ancient mythology with Luna, was supposed to have all the secret powers of nature at her command. In fact, the High Priestess corresponds to all the virgin goddesses of the ancient world – to Artemis, guardian and helper of childbirth, to Maia, mother of Hermes, to Bona Dea, who "out of modesty never left her bower, or let herself be seen of men," and to Kybele, whose sanctuaries were caves. Mr. Waite says "she is the spiritual Bride and Mother, the daughter of the stars . . . the Queen of the borrowed light, but this is the light of all." Thus she also represents Eve, before her union with Adam.

Her number, 2, has been explained hitherto. As a symbol of duplication, reflection, copying, transcription, reproduction, and so on, it relates definitely to memory, and memory is the basic function of the subjective mind. The number 2 also suggests the ideas of duplicity, deception, untruth, illusion, error and delusion. This again is correct, because the subjective mind repeats and elaborates the mistaken results of faulty, superficial self–conscious observation. Being at all times uncritically amenable to suggestion, and at the same time the channel of telepathic communication, it is the source of most of the foolish notions which cause our maladjustments. Something of this lies behind the Bible allegory of Eve being the means of Adam's temptation and fall.

In contrast to the Magician, who stands upright in a garden, the High Priestess is seated within the precincts of a temple. The walls of the building are blue, and so are the vestments of the High Priestess. Blue is the color assigned to the Moon and to water in the color scale of certain Western occult schools. It is the color of the primary root substance, the cosmic mind stuff, which is the element particularly attributed to the Creative World. It has already been intimated that the High Priestess herself is a symbol of this root substance.

The two pillars between which she sits are those of Solomon and Hermes. Opposite in color, but alike in form, they represent affirmation (*J* or Jachin) and negation (*B* or Boaz). For strength (Boaz) is rooted in resistance or inertia, which is the negation of the activity that is the establishing principle (Jachin) of all things. The High Priestess sits between the pillars, because she is the equilibrating power between the *Yes* and *No*, the initiative and the resistance, the light and the darkness.

Alike in form, close to each other, opposite in color, the pillars represent three laws of the association of ideas and of memory. We associate things similar, things near together in space or time, things sharply contrasted.

The veil between the pillars hints that the High Priestess is virgo intacta. It is a phallic symbol of virginity, but is embroidered with palms (male) and pomegranates (female), as if to suggest the union of positive and negative forces. The subjective mind is only potentially reproductive. It is, however, like a veil or covering for the subconscious. Only when the veil is rent or penetrated by concentrated suggestions may the creative activities of the subconsciousness be released and actualized.

The crown is blue–white, like silver, metal of the Moon. It also shows the crescents of the waxing and waning Moon, with her full orb between. This is the horned diadem of the Egyptian Isis, another of the feminine deities personifying the root–matter of all things.

She sits on a cubic stone, a symbol of salt, which crystallizes in perfect cubes, and a reminder of the saltiness of that mystical sea which is associated with the Virgin Mary. Since the time of Pythagoras, moreover, it has been taught openly that the cube is the regular solid representing *earth*, or actual material manifestation. Thus the High Priestess sits on a cube because the basis of all subjective mental activity is what has actually happened, what actually exists. Again, a cube has 6 sides, 8 points, 12 boundary lines. The numbers required to express its peculiar limitations are 6, 8, and 12, whose sum, 26, is the number of the word

IHVH. What actually exists, what really is, what materialists and idealists alike misunderstand and misinterpret, is the real presence of That which was, is and shall be. That real presence is the basis of all subjective mental activity.

The robe of the High Priestess is blue–white, suggesting coldness and moisture, the astrological properties of the Moon, and the characteristics of water. Its folds, moreover, show a shimmering radiance, like that of moonlight on water. This garment seems to flow out of the picture, like a stream. It symbolizes the *stream of consciousness* mentioned in books of psychology. In the Tarot it is the source of the river and of the pools which appear in several subsequent major trumps.

The scroll is that of memory. In some versions of the Tarot it is a book, half–open. This is the record of past events, of all mental and physical states, recorded by the subjective mind. Subjective mind, like all other states of consciousness, is both universal and personal. Thus the memory record includes the past events of race–history, the past events of the history of the planet, the past events of this whole cycle of cosmic manifestation. On this account the scroll is inscribed with the word *TORA*, the phonetic equivalent of the Hebrew *Torah*, or *Law*; Natural law is the cosmic subjective record of all the Life power's self–expressions.

The lunar crescent at her feet repeats the symbolism of her crown, and confirms the attribution of the picture to the letter Gimel. It is colored yellow, to suggest the reflection of the yellow, Mercurial light which the subjective mind reflects from the influence of the descending power of impressions received from the self–conscious plane.

The solar cross on the High Priestess' breast shows the union of positive (upright) and negative (horizontal), male and female, active and passive, originating and duplicating elements. It also symbolizes and foreshadows the number 4, as do the square sides of the cube.

THE EMPRESS

D aleth (ד, D, value 4) originally signified the leaf of a door – that which admits or bars; but it also symbolizes that through which something passes. On this account some writers say Daleth represents the womb, as the door of life. The door itself, then, suggests defense, protection, preservation, safekeeping, conservation and related ideas. This is a clue to the mode of consciousness that is represented by Daleth. We shall find that it is that which has much to do with personal safety, with self–preservation, with defense against trouble and disease, and with the conservation and storage of all that is useful to us. The idea of passage suggested by the doorway brings to mind both ingress and egress, motion into and motion out from. It also suggests transmission, diffusion, dissemination, separation (as when one thinks of a door as the means of leaving a house), and so division, apportionment, partition, or administration. We shall find, too, that these ideas are definitely connected with the mode of consciousness connected with Daleth.

Venus is the planetary attribution. She corresponds to the Egyptian goddess Hathor (whose name, in old manuscripts, is occasionally spelled ATOR). Venus presides over childbirth, is a mother–goddess, and patroness of love, beauty and art. Astrologers say that Venus rules the sense of touch, and has much influence upon the disposition. In the color scale here used, Venus is green, and corresponds to F–sharp or G–flat in the musical scale.

Wisdom and Folly is the pair of opposites, because the mode of consciousness attributed to Daleth is the subconsciousness, and subconscious response to self–conscious interpretation and suggestion determines whether our ideas (mental offspring) are wise or foolish. The occult meanings of Daleth indicate clearly that this letter corresponds to subconsciousness. The latter has no power of inductive reasoning, but its powers of deduction are practically perfect. Now, the very word deduction means *leading away from*, and this kind of reasoning is separative in quality, because it splits up an original premise into an indefinite number of particular consequences or applications. Whether the conclusions so reached shall be wise or foolish depends entirely upon the soundness of the initial premise. The latter is formulated by self–conscious observation and inductive reasoning. If it is accurate and profound, the subconscious subdivisions and elaborations of the premise will be on the side of wisdom. If it is inexact and superficial, the subconscious developments will be on the side of folly.

East, the direction assigned to Daleth, is the door whereby the sun enters the world at the beginning of the day. It is the place of the birth of light. This refers to the fact that the subconsciousness is the womb of those ideas which enlighten the world. In Hebrew the noun for East is אור, AVR (pronounced *our*), and the noun for Light has the same spelling and practically the same pronunciation.

Luminous Intelligence, the phase of consciousness represented by Daleth, requires little explanation after the preceding. Subconsciousness enlightens us by its deductions from our observations. Those deductions are not only illuminating, but also make for our safety, self–preservation, welfare. Again, they enable us to share in the administration of our environment, assure us of our just portion of all good things, and enable us to find a way out of the limitations and bondage that imprison the unenlightened in the cage built by their own ignorance and misunderstanding.

The Empress means literally, *She who sets in order.* She is the feminine ruling power. She is also supposedly a mother, wife of an emperor. Her name contrasts with *High Priestess,* which indicates the cold virginity of a cloistered devotee of the gods. In like manner, mythology contrasts the warm mother goddess, Venus, with Diana, virgin goddess of the Moon.

The scene is a rich, fertile garden. In the background are cypress trees, sacred to Venus. Ripening wheat in the foreground is sacred to Isis–Hathor, also to Ceres, another mother goddess. For this picture, primarily representing Venus or Hathor, is also a symbol of other mythological representations of Mother Nature.

The stream and pool in the background correspond to the stream of consciousness which has its source in the robe of the High Priestess. The symbol of water falling into a pool is also a subtle intimation of the union of male and female modes of the cosmic energy. For the stream is modified and directed by the self–conscious activities represented by the Magician, and the pool represents the accumulation of these self–conscious influences in subconsciousness. This stream waters the garden and makes it fertile.

The Empress is a matronly figure. She has yellow hair (radiant energy) bound by a green wreath of myrtle. This wreath has the same general meaning as that around the head of the Fool. Myrtle, moreover, is a plant sacred to Venus. The idea here conveyed is that the growth and organization of the plant–world is the work of the cosmic energy operating at subconscious levels. This is literally true, and people who know how to reach the subconsciousness in plants can do almost anything with them. Luther Burbank is an outstanding example. But there are other methods than his. Growing plants respond to curses and blessings, and people who love flowers most are usually most successful with them.

The Empress is crowned with twelve stars, like the woman in the Apocalypse. (Rev. Xxi. 1). The stars are six–pointed, to show that she has dominion over the laws of the Macrocosm, or great world. This crown of twelve stars also represents the Zodiac, the year and time, like the Fool's girdle.

52

Venusian symbols abound in this picture: pearls around the Empress's neck, the unit of design in the ornamentation of her dress, the yellow figures on one of the pillows, and finally, the astrological symbol of Venus on a heart–shaped shield beside her. *Heart* in practical occultism means subconsciousness. In some old versions of the picture the shield bears a dove, a bird sacred to Venus. Note that the circular part of the astrological symbol is green.

"The sceptre which she bears," according to Mr. Waite, "is surmounted by the globe of this world." Thus it implies dominance over the conditions of the physical plane. It is also a variation of the symbol on the shield for the handle of the sceptre is twice as long as the diameter of the globe surmounting it. The occult meaning is derived from the geometrical meaning of a circle and its two diameters. The circle occultly means 22 and since the diameters form a cross, they represent the number 4. Thus a circle and cross combine the numbers 22 and 4, whose sum is 26, or IHVH – That which was, is and shall be.

Psychologically the Empress represents subconsciousness. She is the mother of ideas, the generatrix of mental images. The power by which she works is the power of subdivision of root ideas into various forms. In reasoning this is the function of subconsciousness called deduction. The apparent multiplication of images is really the splitting up of root ideas into manifold presentations. She is called the Empress because subconsciousness has direct control over all the sequences of development in the material world. Occult science declares that this control extends even to the mineral kingdom, so that adepts in the direction of subconsciousness by suggestion are able to produce transformations even in the inorganic world. The particular mental function peculiar to subconsciousness is imagination.

THE EMPEROR

Heh (ה, H as in *honor*, or *E*, value 5) is pronounced *hay*. It means *window*, (literally, wind door.) A window admits light (knowledge) and air (Life Breath, spirit) into the house (Beth) of personality. It also permits outlook, survey, supervision, control, and so on. The most important thing about a window is transparency, and the consideration of this takes us back to the mode of consciousness attributed to the Magician.

Sight is the function attributed to Heh. Vision, inspection, reconnaissance, watchfulness, care, vigilance, examination, calculation, analysis, induction, inquiry, investigation, and the like, are all associated in thought and language. Thus we may expect to find the mode of consciousness associated with this letter one which is active in this kind of mental operations.

Constituting Intelligence is the name given it in the Hebrew wisdom, and it is said to "constitute creation in the darkness of the world." To constitute is to make anything what it is, to frame, to compose. Constitution is closely related to authorship. The author of anything is its producer, originator, inventor, founder, generator, architect and builder. Authorship, likewise, is closely connected in our thought with paternity, and paternal authority depends upon the fact that the father is the founder of the family.

In this connection it is interesting to find that the letter Heh is used in Hebrew precisely as we employ the English definite article *the*. The Constituting Intelligence is the defining consciousness. This shows us, first of all, that it is a variant of self–conscious activity, because to define anything is to name it, and we have already associated self–consciousness with Adam, the namer. Definition, moreover, limits, sets boundaries, circumscribes. It specializes, particularizes, enters into detail, and makes distinctions. The qualities thus indicated are precisely those which enter into the making of a constitution for any form of society (and that the constitution is the supreme authority in that particular social organization). Thus the letter ה, *Heh,* as the definite article implies regulation, order, law, and all related ideas. Laws are definitions, and it should always be borne in mind that what we call the laws of nature are simply definitions or descriptions of the sequence of events in some particular field of observation. What is even more important for the occultist and psychologist is that our personal definitions of the meaning of existence constitute suggestions which are accepted without reservation by the subconsciousness. Thus, in a sense, every man makes his own law, writes the constitution of his own personal world, and his life experience is the reproduction of that constitution through the subconscious responses.

Heh is the first of the twelve *simple* letters of the Hebrew alphabet, so called because each has but a single pronunciation. To it is attributed the first sign of the zodiac, Aries, the Ram. Aries is a fiery, cardinal sign. It governs the head and face. It is ruled by Mars, significant of force, strength, energy, courage and activity. Mars rules iron, steel, surgery, chemistry and military affairs. The Sun is exalted (raised to its highest degree of expression) in Aries. It has much to do with health and vitality. It is the significator of high office, positions of rank and title, and so represents rulership and authority. Its metal is gold. Aries is a scientific and philosophical sign, and this agrees with all that has been said about the Constituting Intelligence, inasmuch as science and philosophy have accurate definition as their basis. Astrologers say that Aries represents rulership, government, guidance and leadership. All this, also, agrees with the ideas which we have found represented by the letter Heh. The color corresponding to Aries is scarlet; the musical tone, C–natural.

North–East is the direction attributed to Heh. It combines North (XVI) with East (III). The Roman numerals in parenthesis refer to the numbers of major trumps in the Tarot. Here they designate the Tower, the trump corresponding to Mars, and the Empress, the trump representing Venus and imagination. Later on, it will be evident that the Constituting Intelligence combines the destruction of the structures of falsehood represented in the sixteenth key with the development of mental images shown by the Empress. Accurate definition is always destructive to error, and always the basis of new developments on the form side of life.

The Emperor means literally *he who sets in order*, and from what has been said it will be seen to be perfectly applicable to this picture. It implies both authority and paternity. It also represents the head of government, the source of law, the war–making power, and so on. These ideas are related to the sign Aries and to Mars and the Sun. They are ideas, moreover, which are in close correspondence with the meanings of the number IV, already given.

The red background of the picture refers to the fiery quality of the sign Aries. It is also the color of the sign itself. Furthermore, it is the color of the planet Mars. Close examination will show that it is mixed with yellow, the Sun's color, as an intimation of the exaltation of that great light in the first sign of the zodiac.

The mountains in the distance are volcanic in appearance, forbidding heights in sharp contrast to the valley where the Empress sits. Barren, they indicate vividly the sterility of mere regulation or supervision, unless there is something vitally warm and fruitful to set in order. At their base flows a river, the same stream of consciousness that we have seen before.

The ram's heads, symbols of Aries, are five in number. Four are on the throne, and one is embroidered on the Emperor's cape. There are five, hinting at the correspondence of the picture to the letter Heh, whose number is also 5.

Like the seat of the High Priestess and the

throne of the Empress, the throne of the Emperor is of stone, showing that the mode of consciousness here symbolized has its seat or basis in laws of cosmic manifestation which are at work in the mineral kingdom. A very few laws suffice for all the complex manifestations of the Life power, and they are at work on *low* planes as well as on *high*.

To design this throne both square and compasses were required, because part of the chair is semicircular. In preparing the stone for it, all the implements of masonry were employed – gavel, level, square, plumb, and so on. Masonic readers of these pages will do well to ponder the correspondences suggested. Others will see that the throne itself represents the order, regularity and preparation associated with the title of the card and with the number IV.

The Emperor's crown is surmounted by a tiny Aries symbol. The crown itself has five divisions visible, composing half the total number. Thus the crown signifies the number 10, which Qabalists call *Kingdom*. The five visible divisions remind us that the number of Heh is 5. The metal of the crown is gold, representing the Sun, exalted in Aries.

In addition to the crown are the sceptre and globe, also of the metal of the sun, and referring to his exaltation in Aries. Crown, sceptre and globe also hint that the work of regulation is a work of light, dependent upon vision, which is the sensory and conscious adaptation of solar radiance. The sceptre is a modified Venus symbol. It is also one form of the Egyptian ankh, or sign of life. Being a cross surmounted by a circle it gives the same numeral formula of IHVH shown by the symbol of Venus. It means that the power of regulation is chiefly derived from the exaltation of the solar energy in the sense of sight and in the mental vision which is the inner correspondence thereto. Among the followers of Pythagoras, the globe or sphere was accounted the most perfect solid. It is therefore the emblem of perfected work.

The Emperor's blue undergarment is like the robe of the High Priestess, because all that he represents is dependent upon memory. His red outer robe repeats the symbolism of the robe of the Magician. Thus the Venusian sceptre and these two garments show that in the Emperor are combined powers derived from the Magician, the High Priestess and the Empress. His cape is, or should be, royal purple, to show by the mixture of red and blue that he expresses himself through a combination of self–conscious (red) and subjective (blue) agencies. His armor is of steel, metal of Mars, and represents not only his war–making power, but also the rulership of Mars in Aries.

He is an old man with a white beard, but he is also identical with the Magician. That is, he is the Magician after the latter's marriage with the High Priestess has made her the Empress, and himself the father of her children. Another reason for his being shown with white hair and beard is that he represents in one sense the

Grand Architect of the Universe, often called *The Ancient of Days.* He is the supreme NOUS, or Reason, the constituting power, alike of the great world and of the little, of the universe and of man. Psychologically, therefore, he represents the self–conscious mental plane, when the activities of that plane are engaged in the work of inductive reasoning whereby error arising from superficial interpretations of experience is overthrown. He is the definer, the law–maker, the regulator. Never forget that this phase of consciousness is the ruling principle in human personality. It frames the constitution of your personal world.

THE HIEROPHANT

Vau (ו, V, U, W, value 6) means *Nail*, or *Hook*; something to join the parts of a building together, therefore associative, like Gimel; also something to support hanging objects, therefore something upon which other things depend. A nail is a fastening, a link, a means of union. As a means of support it is linked in thought and language with such ideas as aid, assistance, sustenance, furtherance and ministry. It will be seen presently that all these ideas are not only directly connected with the occult meanings of Vau, but also with the symbolism of the Hierophant.

In the Hebrew language the letter Vau is the equivalent of English *and.* Thus the grammatical use of the letter is derived directly from its literal meaning. *And* is a conjunction, serving to introduce dependent clauses in a sentence. Thus, like a nail, it binds the parts of a sentence together, and clauses or phrases introduced by it hang from it, like pictures supported by hooks driven into a wall.

Now, the central thought suggested here is *union*, and this is the exact English translation of the Sanskrit noun *yoga.* This noun, moreover, is the root of the word *yoke,* and some authorities are of the opinion that the original hieroglyphic symbol for Vau was a yoke such as is used in harnessing oxen. Yoga is a system of practice

63

whereby the personal consciousness is linked to the universal conscious energy. Its object is direct, firsthand experience of those phases of reality which are the basis of all religions. The founders of religions are people who have such experiences, and the contention of practical occultists is that this kind of experience is repeatable – that it is not miraculous. We shall find, presently, that the Hierophant represents the mode of conscious activity whose highest aspects take form in such experiences.

Hearing, which unites man to man by speech, and man to God by the Word of the Inner Voice, is the function attributed to Vau. Jesus often said, "He that hath ears to hear, let him hear." This is a technical formula of Ageless Wisdom. It refers to the development of the interior sense of hearing just mentioned. In Sanskrit the noun *sruti*, literally *hearing*, is the term for revelation. "It alone can remove that nescience which is innate in human nature," says one ancient book. Similarly, the prophets of Israel say, again and again, "Thus saith the Lord," as if they were reporting things heard. Two of them, Samuel and Elijah, were directly aware of the Divine Presence as a Voice. What was true then is true now. Knowledge of the higher aspects of reality comes to us through the soundless sound of an Inner Voice, which often speaks as plainly as any voice heard with the physical ear. The reason is that the hearing centers in the brain are stimulated by higher rates of vibration which serve as a means of communication between ourselves and more advanced thinkers. Many people have flashes of this experience, as is shown by the oft–repeated statement, "Something seemed to say to me."

Triumphant and Eternal Intelligence is the Hebrew name of the mode of consciousness. It is *Triumphant* because it gives assurance of the ultimate victory of the Life power over all apparent obstacles now seeming to stand in the way of the completion of the Great Work. It is *Eternal* because it not only carries with it a positive conviction of immortality, but also lifts personal consciousness out of the limitations of Time into the realization of the freedom of Eternity.

Taurus, the Bull, a fixed, earthly sign, is attributed to Vau. It is ruled by the planet Venus (III, the Empress), and is the sign of the exaltation of the Moon (II, the High Priestess). The name of the sign itself shows a secret correspondence with spiritual things, inasmuch as Aleph, the Bull, is the letter representing Ruach, the Life Breath. Astrologically, too, the sign Taurus is representative of latent powers and energies, of secretiveness and reserve – ideas clearly suggested by the title and symbolism of the Hierophant. Furthermore, Taurus rules the neck, which is the link between the head and the body; and in the neck is located a certain psychic center dominated by the Venus vibration. The exaltation of the Moon, or High Priestess, in Taurus indicates that memory has its highest manifestation in this phase of the Life power's self–expression. In our color scale, Taurus is red–orange. Its note is C–sharp or D–flat.

South–East, the direction attributed to Vau, combines the ideas of South (XIX, the Sun) with those of East (III, the Empress). Here is suggested a blending of the solar and Venusian qualities. The Sun is the great center of what Hindus call Prana. The Venusian vibration is that which manifests in mental imagery. Occultly, the blending of the two vibrations is the mingling of the universal Conscious Energy with the imaginative, generative powers of subconsciousness. The Sun here typifies superconsciousness, and Venus is the subconsciousness. In the activities represented by the Hierophant, these two phases of the Life power are combined.

Hierophant means *revealer of mysteries.* It was the name of the chief officer in the Eleusinian mysteries, and signifies that which makes known the hidden import of the appearances whereby we are surrounded. In many versions of the Tarot this trump is called *The Pope,* but Mr. Waite rightly says that this is "a particular application of the more general office that he symbolizes." I do not agree with Mr. Waite that "he is the ruling power of external religion . . . exoteric orthodox doctrine . . . the outer side of the life which leads to the doctrine." He is the pontifix, or *bridge maker* who provides a connecting link between outer experience and interior illumination.

The background is gray, a color associated in occultism with Wisdom – the equal balance of the known (white) and unknown (black).

The pillars are of stone, like the thrones of the High Priestess, Empress and Emperor, suggesting that the support of the temple of wisdom is the law which obtains even in the mineral kingdom. The design on the capitals of the pillars is a phallic symbol of union. The pillars themselves repeat the motif of duality, and suggest the laws of association represented by the pillars of the High Priestess.

The throne is also of stone, with the same meaning. At the back of the throne, on either side of the Hierophant's head is a cleverly concealed astrological symbol of Taurus.

The crown is a triple tiara, like the Pope's crown. Above it in black is the letter W, equivalent to Vau. The crown is of gold, symbolizing radiant energy and wisdom. It is ornamented with three rows of trefoils: top row, 3; middle row, 7; bottom row, 5. The total number is 15, number of the Hebrew god–name יה, IH, *Jah*, particularly associated with Wisdom. Since the trefoils also symbolize the number 3, fifteen of them represent 3 x 15, or 45, number of the name אדם, ADM, *Adam*. The three in the upper row designate the threefold nature of the Life power; the seven in the second row represent its sevenfold expression (recognized in all occult schools, and called in the Bible the Seven Spirits of God); the five in the bottom row stand for the five modes of its manifestation in the material world (the four *elements* and the Quintessence, also the five senses of man).

Vestments: White undergarment like that of the Fool and the Magician, with same meanings. Blue middle robe, visible at neck and feet, is same as that of the High Priestess and Emperor. Red outer robe like that of the Magician and Emperor. The white pallium is a combination of circle and line, the line being twice the diameter of the circle, so that it is a Venus symbol concealed. The three crosses on the line of the pallium refer to the three higher of the four worlds. The little circle with four projecting points designates the material world. Crosses on the Hierophant's shoes refer to the union of male and female, positive and negative, forces, and to the order (4, cross) that results from that union.

Sceptre: Golden, to suggest radiant energy, or adaptation of the Life power. Three cross–bars are the three lower worlds (material, formative and creative). The round knob at the top is the archetypal world. The sceptre symbolizes power or dominion (staff) extending through all four worlds.

Sign of esotericism (gesture of the right hand): Signifies *Three revealed and two concealed.* The three revealed are the three dimensions we know. The two concealed are the fourth and fifth dimensions. The fourth is that in which every direction is at right angles to our three dimensions. The fifth is that in which all directions and dimensions are summarized into a single archetypal point. This will convey little meaning to persons who have not had metaphysical or super conscious experience. Yet the general significance of the gesture is plain. What you see is only part of the total *Reality*. It is the negation of materialism.

Square dais: Suggests the number 4 and measurement, as if to indicate that however far beyond our present experience higher consciousness may go, it rests upon a solid basis of fact and reason. The dais is covered with a carpet which should be red orange in color, to correspond to the sign Taurus. Four circles on it enclose crosses – the Venus symbol folded in upon itself. They represent the manifestation of IHVH in the four worlds. Black and white checkerwork on the carpet is reminiscent of the Masonic mosaic pavement. It represents the alternation of light and darkness in the manifestation of the Life power.

Keys: Golden, to suggest light. Their handles show the cross and circle of IHVH. On close examination their wards show the *bell and clapper* design. This implies that the keys to control have something to do with sound vibration (hearing). The design is also a familiar phallic symbol of union. They are the keys to heaven and hell, to creation and destruction.

Ministers: Their robes repeat the motif of the flowers in the Magician's garden. Their yellow palliums are symbols of the yoke, or union. Yellow, because the yoke is that of Mercury, or intellectual perception. The one who wears lilies personifies thought, the other represents desire. Their attitude of attentive listening refers to hearing.

The number of this trump, as you have learned, is that of Law, of adaptation, of religion, and of man. Psychologically the Hierophant represents Intuition, which follows reasoning, and adds to it. Intuition is the subjective response to reason, whereby through the laws of association at work in the subjective mind, thought–relations which go beyond the results attained by self–conscious reason are perceived. They are perceived usually by interior hearing. Intuition, it should be noted, means literally *inner tuition.*

THE LOVERS

Zain (ז, Z, value 7) means *sword* or *weapon*, suggesting the antithesis of Vau, the nail, because a sword cleaves, cuts, divides, separates. Diversity, contrast, antithesis, distinction, and therefore discrimination are some of the related ideas. Discrimination implies nice perception, acuteness (sharpness, like a sword's edge), sagacity, and so on.

Smell has been always the sense associated with keen perception and sagacity. An old Qabalistic maxim says: "Properties are discerned by the nose." Our everyday speech has a number of phrases like *smell out* to suggest approach to truth.

East–Above combines East (III, Empress) with Above (I, Magician). Here is intimated a combination of the subconscious powers of imagination with the conscious power of acute discrimination.

Gemini, the Twins, is the zodiacal sign attributed to Zain. The name of the sign suggests duality, division, and other ideas related to the meaning of the letter. It is difficult to tell twins apart, and to do so requires nice discrimination. The sign Gemini is ruled by Mercury (I, Magician), sometimes personified in Egyptian mythology as the jackal–headed Anubis, representing discernment and sagacity because of the jackal's keen sense of smell. Gemini rules the lungs, collarbones, shoulders, arms and hands (all in pairs). Gemini people are said by astrologers to be given to inquiry, investigation and experimenting. They usually engage in more or less mental pursuits. In our color scale, Gemini is represented by the color orange. Its musical tone is D–natural. It is a common sign, of the airy triplicity.

Disposing Intelligence: To dispose is literally *to place apart*, to arrange, distribute, apportion, or divide. Thus analysis (also implied by the meanings of the letter name, sword), classification, organization, preparation and adjustment are all related to this mode of consciousness. This it is which shows itself in our *disposition*, and one's disposition can be modified by right discrimination.

The Lovers is the more common title. Some pseudo–occultists call this picture *The Two Paths*, and say older versions of the symbolism represent a man standing between Virtue and Vice. This is wholly erroneous. In old Tarots the design has obvious reference to marriage. The title intimates the union of opposite but complimentary modes of existence. It is also closely related to *Disposing Intelligence*.

Disposition, affections, temperament, idiosyncrasy, propensities – all these are related to the word *love*, as well as to the occult meaning of the Tarot trump now under consideration.

Ancient versions show a young man and young woman, standing with clasped hands before an older crowned woman. The analysis of this design requires a great deal of special information about the details of Hebrew Wisdom. Mr. Waite's revision of the symbolism is true to the essential meanings, and easier for the average person to read.

The sun overhead has the same general significance as that behind the Fool. It is the great light source, the dynamo of radiant energy whence all creatures derive their personal forces. Here it is yellow instead of white, showing that it is our day star, the actual physical sun whence we draw not only energy and life, but also, says the Ageless Wisdom, potential consciousness. The sun is not merely a center of physical force, a thing in the sky. It is the body of a Being.

The angel is Raphael, angel of air, the element attributed to the sign Gemini. He is also the great archangel of the Eastern quarter of the heavens (East Above), and he corresponds in occultism to Mercury, ruler of Gemini. Here he represents superconsciousness, and thus is related also to the Fool. His airy nature is indicated by the color of his skin, the yellow we have associated with air and Mercury. His violet garment carries out the same idea, because violet is the color–complement of yellow. Another indication of his airy nature is the fact that he is supported by clouds. He is the cosmic Life Breath, Prana, superconsciousness. His influences descend on both figures below, streaming from his upraised hands.

Mountain: Mountains are symbols of the dwelling–place of the gods. Consider Sinai, Olympus, Meru, and Fujiyama. Again, they suggest climbing, aspiration, and the possibility of attainment. We all have peaks to climb, and the incentive to action, the disposing element in consciousness which leads to volition, has always in the background this idea of climbing above our present level. Again, a mountain is often a phallic symbol of pregnancy, or gestation, suggesting preparation, organization, and similar ideas which have already been developed in connection with the letter name Zain.

The Man is Adam, namer of things and tiller of the soil. He is also the Magician. Behind him is a tree bearing twelve fiery fruits. These are the twelve signs of the zodiac. Thus the tree behind the man is the tree of human existence, and its fruits represent the twelve main types of self–conscious life expression.

The Woman is Eve. She is also the High Priestess and the Empress. Behind her is the Tree of Knowledge of Good and Evil. It bears five circular, red fruits – the five senses. Up the tree climbs the serpent of sensation, because temptation arises from subjective memory of sensation, or from suggestions based thereon. The serpent is also the symbol of wisdom and redemption (Moses' serpent in the wilderness), because wisdom and liberation result from the right adaptation of the very forces which at first tempt us into mistaken action. Thus Mr. Waite says: "The suggestion in respect of the woman is that she signifies that attraction towards the sensitive life which carries within it the idea of the Fall of Man, but she is rather the working of a Secret Law of Providence than a willing and conscious temptress. It is through her imputed lapse that man shall rise ultimately, and only by her can he complete himself."

In practical psychology the lesson of the picture is plain. The woman looks toward the angel, the man toward the woman. The self-conscious intellectual mind, although it is the determining factor in personal consciousness, does not become directly aware of superconsciousness, although it transmits and receives its influences. Awareness comes through the channel of subconscious activities. Powers are developed within (the woman), but they are educated or drawn forth from without (the man). Development comes by response of the inner to the outer. It is the answer of woman to man that peoples the world. It is the response of the interpreting subconsciousness to the observing self-consciousness that peoples the thought–world with ideas. This is the great law of mental development. Its constructive operation depends upon the discriminative exercise of self–conscious mental powers.

Personal happiness, health and success depend upon harmonious cooperation of these two modes of mental activity. To secure this harmony, we must understand that both are expressions of a power superior to either. We must also see that subconsciousness is the

mode which in response to suggestions origi-
nated and framed by self–consciousness brings
us into personal relationship with this superior
power.

Furthermore, the relationship between self–
consciousness and subconsciousness should be
one of loving intimacy. Hence the two figures
are nude. They veil nothing from each other.
This is not the state of affairs with most people.
Subconsciousness and self–consciousness are
commonly "not on speaking terms." Consciously we accept an idea. Subconsciously we seek
the realization of its opposite. To correct this
error, to establish harmony between these two
phases of personality, is to have clear, definite,
unmixed, unadulterated desires.

Finally, since love is the ideal relation between
the two modes of consciousness, this picture
warns us against all attempts to bully or coerce
subconsciousness by wrong methods in giving
suggestions. Persuade subconsciousness, and it
will do anything for you. Drive it harshly, and
you set into operation the law of reversed effort,
so that you get just the opposite of what you are
aiming at.

Discrimination, then, is the key to right relations of the two modes of personal consciousness. The burden falls upon self–consciousness,
because it is the framer of suggestion. If it is
careless and lax in observation, harsh and driv-
ing in giving commands to the subconscious,
the results are destructive. On the other hand,
if self–conscious intellect perceives the true re-

lation between the three modes of consciousness, as set forth in this picture, it can frame a suggestion which will make it the recipient of super conscious guidance, through the agency of the subconscious. All that is necessary is to formulate a suggestion embodying the idea that the subconscious is indeed the means of such guidance. The exact form of words chosen must be your own. Study the picture, and endeavor to embody its meaning into a formula of auto–suggestion. You will be amazed and delighted at the result.

THE CHARIOT

C heth (ח, Ch, and H as in *help*, value 8) is pronounced *khayth.* It means a fence and the field enclosed thereby.

Fence suggests enclosure, protection, defense; specific location; an area set apart for cultivation. It also implies shielding, safeguard, refuge, shelter; and thus corresponds to the ideas represented by the words carapace and shell.

The idea of location refers back to *house,* or Beth, as does that of shelter. Cultivation is likewise represented by the Magician's garden. Furthermore, the enclosure of a particular area by a fence is exactly what happens when we define anything, so that Cheth is also a reflection of Heh, considered as the definite article.

Speech is definitive. Words are fences enclosing particular fields of consciousness. The field of speech continually engages the labors of the practical occultist and the applied psychologist. The attribution of speech to Cheth, therefore, indicates that words have a preservative and protective power, that right use of language is a means of safety. Extend the meaning of speech from the spoken words to the unspoken words of thought, and you will begin to understand why it is so important.

Intelligence of the House of Influence means literally, *consciousness of that which is the abode of inflowing power.* Specifically, it is consciousness of the fact that human personality is a fenced–in area wherein universal forces are at work. These forces flow into personality from beyond its boundaries. Taking form in the silent speech of thought, and finding utterance in the spoken word, they flow out through personality into actual expression and manifestation.

East–Below is a direction combining East (III, Empress) and Below (II, High Priestess). Here is intimation that although self–conscious elements are involved, the activities we are now considering are principally those of the subjective and subconscious planes of mentation. A little self–study will convince you that your thought and speech are largely subjective and subconscious in their makeup. Your vocabulary depends upon the subjective associative processes. Your sentences, your style, your figures of speech – all these are framed in your subconsciousness.

Cancer, the Crab, a cardinal, watery sign, is attributed to the letter Cheth. Here we see the connection between the letter name, *fence*, and the crab's hard carapace or shell. Cancer is ruled by the Moon (II, High Priestess), and the planet Jupiter (X, Wheel of Fortune) is said to be exalted therein. Cancer governs the breast, the chest (a fence of bones) and the stomach. Cancer is a psychic, receptive sign, and its natives are said by astrologers to be endowed with exceptionally tenacious memory. All this is in accordance with the basic ideas of the letter name. In our color scale, the tint assigned to

Cancer is orange–yellow. Its musical tone is D-sharp or E–flat.

The Chariot is the usual title. Sometimes it is *The Charioteer,* which is even better, since the picture, as Mr. Waite says, is really "the King in his triumph, typifying, however, the victory which creates kingship as its natural consequence." Note, in this connection, that the number of the card, VII, is that to which Hebrew wisdom assigns the idea of Victory.

In the background is a walled city. The wall is a stone fence. The city is a collection of houses, suggesting the ideas behind the letter Beth and the Magician. The windows of some of the buildings are clearly shown, indicating that what is represented by Heh and the Emperor is also behind the surface meanings of this picture. But the wall is what specially establishes the correspondence of this trump to Cheth, the Fence.

Trees and a river in the middle distance remind us of the symbolism of the Empress. This is correct because Speech is not only composed of definitions, but also embodies mental imagery (Empress) and gives form to the stream of consciousness. As the river is primarily, in the Tarot, the watery substance of the robe of the High Priestess, and as trees are associated with the rich fertility of the Empress's garden, here, too, is the combination suggested by East–Below (East, Empress and below, High Priestess.

The chariot itself is a movable fence, corresponding to the letter Cheth. Its body is a cube, symbolizing existence and the name IHVH. Surmounting it are four pillars. Their number is that of order and measurement. It is also the number of the laws of association represented in the symbolism of the pillars and scroll of the High Priestess. These pillars support a starry canopy, representing the sum total of planetary, zodiacal and human forces. Planetary forces are symbolized by eight–pointed stars, referring particularly to the influence of the fixed stars, because an eight–pointed star is always a sun–symbol, and the fixed stars are really suns. Six–pointed stars on the canopy refer to zodiacal forces, because the hexagram is the basis of the geometrical construction of the wheel of the zodiac used in astrology. Five–pointed stars, or pentagrams, refer to the number 5, and to the human forces used in adapting cosmic laws to personal applications. Thus the stars on the azure canopy suggest the correlation of the influences of distant suns and planets, of zodiacal constellations, and of human forces. Human forces and stellar influences are of the same basic nature and quality – as modern science demonstrates repeatedly with every advance in physics and chemistry.

This starry canopy is connected with the cubical body of the chariot by the four pillars before mentioned. The idea is that orderly associations of ideas are the means whereby the influences of distant centers of the cosmic radiance are linked with its actual manifestation here on the physical plane.

The yellow wheels of the chariot refer to light–energy, but particularly to the specific activities associated in the Tarot with the planet Jupiter, which is said to be exalted in Cancer. This planet is represented in the Tarot by the tenth major trump, called *The Wheel of Fortune.* Jupiter, astrologers say, rules the circulation of the blood, because it really governs all forms of rotation or circular movement.

On the face of the chariot is a shield, emphasizing the ideas of protection and shelter conveyed by the letter name, the wall in the background, and the chariot itself. The red symbol on the shield is the Hindu lingam–yoni, representing the union of positive and negative forces in action (red). In some old Tarots the shield bears the letters .V.T, written with the periods at the left of the letters, to show that they are to be read like Hebrew, from right to left. So read, they spell in Roman letters the Hebrew word תֹו, TV, *Tau.* This is the name of the last letter of the Hebrew alphabet. To an occultist it conveys the same fundamental meaning as does the Hindu lingam–yoni, because Tau is the cross, similar to that on the breast of the High Priestess.

Above the shield is a winged sun, an Egyptian symbol of spiritual energy. The sun disk is yellow, suggesting self–consciousness, because this is the color in our color scale of the planet Mercury, the Magician. The wings are blue, like the robe of the High Priestess. They are symbols of aspiration. The sphinxes which draw the chariot are an innovation suggested by

Eliphas Levi. Older Tarots show horses, which are sometimes joined together like equine Siamese twins. The horses are sun–symbols. The sphinxes, combining animal and human attributes, suggest a force common to men and animals. Their contrasting colors are like the contrast between the pillars of the High Priestess. By mythological allusion, they represent the senses, which are continually propounding riddles. Note that here they are shown at rest, in accordance with the idea of rest attributed to the number VII in Hebrew occultism.

The charioteer is crowned, like the Emperor, but with a diadem whereon blazes an eight–pointed star, symbol of solar energy. His hair is fair, like that of the Empress and Fool, and bound, like theirs, with a green wreath. On his shoulders are lunar crescents, indicating the rulership of the Moon (High Priestess) in Cancer. His cuirass is greenish–yellow, or brass–color, to show that it is made of the metal of Venus (brass or copper). On it a white square, symbolizing the number 4 with its ideas of order, regulation, calculation, and so forth, represents also by its color the purification of matter. His golden belt suggests light, and is embroidered with indistinct signs like those of the zodiac and planets. It represents Time and the influences of stellar forces. His black skirt is marked out in eight divisions, in each of which are shown the geomantic figures employed in making magical talismans or pentacles. They typify dominion over the earth–forces. His sceptre is a blue wand, tipped with a yellow lozenge. The wand itself is a masculine symbol, but its color is that which we have learned to associate with feminine powers. The lozenge is a feminine sign but its color is masculine. Here is an intimation of the interchange and mingling of powers. The sharp point of the wand also suggests concentration.

The charioteer, moreover, is in armor, like the Emperor. Everything about him suggests that he sums up all the powers and potencies of the personages who have preceded him in the series of major trumps. He is a synthesis of them all. He is the true Self, the Master power behind all forms of life expression. Hence Mr. Waite tells us: "He has led captivity captive; he is conquest on all planes – in the mind, in science, in progress in certain trials on initiation... He is above all things triumph in the mind."

His chariot, as we have seen, is a movable fence, and thus it, rather than the driver, is particularly related to the letter name, Cheth, and its meanings. It is the combination of celestial and terrestrial forms of the One Energy. It is drawn by the senses. Its body is identical with that which is the seat of the High Priestess, or the basis of all subjective mental activity. In a word, the chariot is the *House of Influence*, the vehicle of the true Self. It is personality, in which are combined the influences of the most distant stellar forces, and the nearest physical forms.

Thus to this picture we assign the psychological idea, Receptivity–Will. The uninitiated believe that their *will* is something originating in personality. The occultist, without in the least denying the fact that free will is part of our equipment, refuses to believe that *personal* free will has any actual existence. All that we mean by *volition* is for the occultist the synthesis of innumerable cosmic influences. Hence we find Jesus declaring: "I can do nothing of myself." And Jacob Boehme writes: "If thou canst, my son, for a while but cease from all thy thinking and willing, then shalt thou hear the unspeakable words of God. . . When thou are quiet and silent, then art thou as God was before nature and creature; thou art that which God then was; thou art that of which he made thy nature and creature: Then thou hearest and seest even with that wherewith God himself saw and heard in thee, before ever thine own willing or thine own seeing began."

The more perfectly we understand that the office of human personality is to serve as the vehicle for cosmic forces, the more freely does the Primal Will behind all manifestation find expression through us. To other people we may seem to have very strong personal will. But practice will by then have convinced us that the strength of our willing is measured by the degree of our willingness to let life find unobstructed manifestation through us.

That willingness takes form in thought and word, and the thought itself is unuttered speech. It is a willingness developed through purposeful concentration. Relaxation of body, passivity of mind, one-pointed attention to the real presence in our personal field of the limitless powers of the whole universe, with progressive freedom in the expression of those powers as our dominant purpose – this is the infallible practical formula for triumph in the mind and elsewhere.

The subconsciousness should be impressed again and again with the suggestion that it is the vehicle of the Universal Will. These suggestions must be based upon reason. We must see that the One Energy enters into all modes of power, celestial and terrestrial. Self-examination must convince us that not the least of our personal actions is anything more or less than a particular manifestation in time and space of some phase of the sum total of cosmic influences. Perfect conceptions of this truth may be impossible at this stage of our mental development, but reasonable ones we may have at a little expense of observation and reason. Subconsciousness is the vehicle through which all plans, ideas, designs, inventions and forces enter into the personal field. Thought and speech are potent in molding subconscious response. And because subconsciousness is also the bodybuilding and body-changing power, suggestions of the type here indicated can eventually make profound alterations in physical structure, so that it becomes able to transform into personal activities cosmic forces whose very existence is unsuspected by the greater number of human beings.

Thorough receptivity is the secret of the most powerful manifestations of will. Receptivity may be increased by control of language. Herein lies the key to all the mighty works of practical occultism, for Eliphas Levi says truly, "All magic is in the will."

STRENGTH

Teth (ט, Th, as in *The*, also *T*, value 9) means *snake*, symbol of what has been known among occultists for ages as the *serpent–power*. This was the power typified by the brazen snake of Moses. It is the astral light of Eliphas Levi, the force designated in Theosophy by the word Fohat. It is cosmic electricity, the universal life principle, the conscious energy which takes form as all things, and builds all things from within. The primary secret of practical occultism is that of the control of this energy in its subhuman forms, through mental means.

The serpent also symbolizes secrecy, subtlety, and wisdom. Thus it is applied in the allegory of Genesis to the tempter, and the Bible calls the Devil the *Old Serpent*. This serpent–power is the source of illusion, and thus the *father of lies*. But when it is controlled it becomes the instrumentality of salvation. Again, because the ancients observed that serpents cast their skin, the snake was taken to be a type of regeneration, transmigration, reincarnation and immortality.

Digestion (literally, feeding) is the function attributed to the letter Teth. This recalls the familiar serpent biting its own tail which we have seen in connection with the picture of the Magician. The *serpent–power* feeds upon itself. Scientifically this is exact. The sum total of the universal conscious energy remains ever the same. It enters into various forms of existence, and these forms feed on each other. Thus the serpents on the caduceus, or wand of Hermes, represent this law of endless transformation and conversion.

North–Above combines North (XVI, the Tower) with Above (I, The Magician). The Tower, as we shall see, represents the planet Mars, and the fiery activity which has for its most obvious manifestation the disintegration of forms, even as the first step in the process of digestion is the breaking up of food in mastication, followed by its further disintegration in the chemistry of the stomach and intestines. This disintegrating activity, under the self–conscious direction of the mental states typified by Mercury and the Magician, is the actual basis of all practical occultism. Until one is intelligent enough to select and digest the proper sorts of food, he is not ready to experiment with the higher laws of control that enable adepts to perform their mighty work. Regulation of diet is at the bottom of practical magic. Corresponding to it, on the principle expressed in the Hermetic axiom, "That which is above is as that which is below," is the right selection and assimilation of mental food.

Leo, the Lion, a fixed sign of fiery quality, is attributed to Teth. It is ruled by the Sun (XIX, The Sun). Leo governs the sides, back and heart in the body of man. It is the sign attributed to the tribe of Judah in Hebrew occultism. Its rulership over the back of man refers primarily to the spine, through which the currents of the serpent–power flow when directed in certain kinds of occult practice. In modern astrology, Leo is said to be the sign of the exaltation of Neptune (XII, the Hanged Man). The color of Leo is yellow. Its musical note is E–natural.

Intelligence of the Secret of All Spiritual Activities is the mode of consciousness attributed to Teth. Here it should be borne in mind that in occultism all activities are spiritual, in the literal sense of *spirit* as the cosmic Life Breath. Part of the secret is the law that all forces and activities whatsoever are transmutations and conversions of the one Conscious Energy. Other phases of it will be touched upon in our analysis of the symbols of the eighth trump.

Strength, the title, is sometimes given as Force, and occasionally, but incorrectly, as Fortitude. It is courage only as courage is derived from conscious knowledge of the law typified. The correct titles, Strength or Force, allude to the fiery Life power which is the source of all human powers.

The yellow background of the picture is in accordance with the color attributed to the sign in our scale. A mountain peak is seen in the distance. It is the same one that is shown between the Lovers, and has the same meanings. In contrast to the urban aspect of the preceding trump, here we see an uninhabited plain. We are on the level of actual existence, but the absence of houses suggests that the conditions symbolized are those of nature, apart from human artifice.

The woman is the same as the Empress, representing subconsciousness and the power of mental generation. Instead of a wreath, she wears a crown of flowers, to suggest the idea that the forces of organic life are at this point nearer to fruition. Over her head is the same horizontal 8 that hovers over the Magician. It has the same meaning. It further intimates that something of the Magician's quality has been transferred to the woman. In short, it indicates the fact that subconsciousness receives the impress of self–conscious mental states, and is modified by self–conscious selectivity and initiative. Even as the outcome of the digestive processes, which are themselves governed by subconsciousness, depends upon conscious selection of food, and conscious attention to the preliminary work of mastication, so does the outcome of subconscious operations in general depend for good or ill upon the selection and direction which are the particular business of the self–conscious plane of mind.

The unornamented white robe of the woman signifies purity in the strictest sense of that word, which means *freedom from mixture.* A chain of roses around her waist is also around the lion's neck, and Mr. Waite says she leads him by it. It signifies artistic adaption (chain) of desire (roses), and hints that the fiery power of the Lion is controlled by our self–conscious modifications and adaptations of emotion and desire.

The lion, as king of beasts, represents all subhuman forces, or states of the cosmic vital electricity. The king represents all his subjects. His color refers to the alchemical Red Lion, symbol of sublimated sulphur. Alchemists say that the purification of sulphur is affected by its amalgamation with Mercury, and this is exactly the idea that is hinted at in the direction North–Above, inasmuch as alchemical *sulphur* and *Mars* are closely related. The lion, of course, is also the symbol of the zodiacal sign Leo.

The woman tames him. Here she shuts his mouth. I prefer the older designs which show her opening it, since *to open the mouth* is to make articulate, to give speech to, and whatever has power of speech is assimilated with humanity and impressed by human thought. When we assimilate the hostile, destructive, dangerous, wild forces in nature to the uses of mankind, we add to those forces the quality of human consciousness. Thus electricity, the flaming thunderbolt, tamed and modified by man is now, as Eliphas Levi predicted, what gives to human speech *a universal reverberation and success.*

The meaning of the picture should now be plain. The Great Secret is the law that subconsciousness is at all times in control of the subhuman orders of cosmic energy. The extent of that control is far greater than usually supposed. All the forces of nature, down to those of the inorganic mineral kingdom, are within range of that subconscious direction. Because this is true all the forces of nature are subject to the adept who has mastered his own emotions and desires.

Subconsciousness always directs the activities of the subhuman forces. This is true whether the action of those forces be hostile or friendly to man. Subconsciousness, in turn, is always amenable to impressions originating at the self-conscious level of human mentation. What matters, therefore, is the kind of pattern we set. Our patterns are determined by self-conscious interpretation of experience. If observation and attention (the Magician) are faulty, superficial, fearful, negative, the sequence of subconscious reactions is destructive. Then the spoken word and unuttered speech of thought (the Chariot) are vehicles for a destructive pattern, and we set wild beasts at our own vitals. Change the pattern, and you change the result. Make it accurate, profound, courageous, and positive. Then you tame the lion, and he becomes your servant. This, indeed, is the secret of all spiritual activities, the secret of strength, and the secret of ultimate mastery. Read and re-read it, and study the picture, until you are sure you grasp its meaning to the full.

THE HERMIT

Yod (, I, J, Y, value 10) means the hand of man. It is the open hand, in contradistinction to Kaph, the closed one, which follows it in the alphabet. It indicates power, means, direction; skill, and dexterity; but is the sign rather of tendency, aptitude, inclination, predisposition or potency than of actual activity. In the religious symbolism of the world the open hand is everywhere and at all times a type of beneficence, and of the freedom of the Supreme Spirit.

Coition is the function assigned to this letter, because personal experience of what it represents is intimate union with the Supreme Self, the true I AM of the cosmos. This experience, intensely blissful, is often compared by occult writers, ancient and modern, to the intense physical ecstasy of the sex embrace. Prudes may quarrel with this comparison. Let them read the Song of Solomon, Sufi mystical poetry, or some of the narratives of Christian mystics.

North–Below combines North (XVI, the Tower) with Below (II, the High Priestess). The reason is that the destruction of error symbolized by the Tower is one of the elements in mystical experience. Furthermore, that experience is dependent upon certain transformations of the Mars–force in the physical body. Again, it is said by many occult writers to be the supreme expression of the subjective powers of memory (High Priestess). When we most perfectly remember ourselves we experience this blissful merging of personal consciousness with the universal.

Virgo, the Virgin, a mutable or common earthly sign, is attributed to Yod. It is ruled by Mercury (I, Magician) and is also the sign in which Mercury is exalted. It is dominated, therefore, by self–conscious initiative, and represents the state in which the highest manifestation of self–consciousness is experienced. This state is what the Bible calls *heaven*. Thus it is said that in heaven there is neither marriage nor giving in marriage. This corresponds to the name of the sign, for Virgo means *virgin*. The reason is that in the state of consciousness we are now discussing, all distinctions of separate personality, and, consequently, all distinctions of sex, are completely obliterated.

Virgo rules the intestines, where digestion is completed, and where the final selection is made between assimilable material and that which is rejected as waste. In certain forms of occult practice, concealed under the veils of alchemy, the assimilation of solar energy from food by the lacteals in the small intestine is enormously increased. To this practice we may refer alchemical references to the First Matter as *virgin's milk*, prepared under the regimen of Mercury; to the process of putrefaction symbolized as a black dragon (the convolutions of the intestines in the darkness of the abdominal cavity); and to the fact that in its visible aspect the First Matter is the thing accounted by all men as the vilest thing on earth. The color of Virgo is yellow–green, corresponding to the note F-natural.

Intelligence of Will is the type of consciousness. "It prepares all created beings, each individually, for the demonstration of the existence of the primordial glory," says a Hebrew commentary. The demonstration is the experience hitherto described, and the primordial glory is that of the Supreme Spirit, known in this experience. The word translated *will* means, primarily, *delight,* and then has the supplementary meanings: *pleasure, intent, purpose, determination, will.* Thus we find that all descriptions of mystical experience agree that it is firsthand knowledge of an ineffable glory, of an unspeakable bliss, and of a very certain and definite, although incommunicable, knowledge of the meaning and tendency of the cosmic Life–process. In this experience the question, *What is this all about?* is settled once and for all. In it, too, the knowledge that there is but one Free Will in the cosmos, of which all things and creatures are the personal expressions, is established forever.

The Hermit is a title referring to a passage in a book of Hebrew Wisdom which says: "Yod is above all (symbolizing the Father), and with him is none other associated." A hermit lives alone, isolated. The picture shows him above all, alone on a snowy mountain–peak.

His white beard shows that he is the *Most Holy*

Ancient One, identified with the Primal Will in Hebrew Wisdom. His gray, cowled robe suggests another name derived from the same occult teaching – *Concealed with all Concealment.* He is the source of all, and yet he is the goal of all endeavors. The whole of practical occultism aims at union of personal consciousness with the Cosmic Will which is the Causeless Cause of all particular manifestations.

The correspondence will be better understood after studying the analogies between IX, number of the Hermit, and O, number of the Fool. The sign which precedes all manifestation is 0; and 9, final figure of the digital series, denotes completion, perfection, realization. The only perfect Being must be the Absolute, and the Absolute is not only No–Thing, but also That which is completely alone (Hermit). Perfection is above and beyond all manifestation. 9 therefore represents the Absolute as the Goal of existence, while 0 typifies it as the Source of all. Consequently, in the Tarot 0 is youth, looking upward, in the morning light; but 9 is a bearded ancient, looking down, at night. The Hermit and the Fool are two aspects of That which is the Foundation (9) of all things. The Hermit is the Ancient One, above all things yet supporting all. He precedes everything, and is forever young (the Fool); yet He will continue when all else is passed away, and He is the term of all our hopes.

He stands in darkness, because what is behind our personifications of the Supreme Reality is dark and incomprehensible to our intellects.

The peak is snow–capped because to us this Ancient One is an abstraction, cold and far removed from the warmth of everyday life. Yet he himself carries his own light, and it is the light of a golden six–rayed star, whose interlaced triangles are themselves symbols of union. The star also hints at the sign Virgo, sixth in the zodiacal series.

Although the Hermit seems to be alone he is really the Way–Shower, lighting the path for climbing multitudes below. He has no need to climb, hence his staff is held in his left hand. The staff itself is one of the implements of the Magician, and corresponds to the archetypal world.

The Causeless Cause seems afar off, and a cold, isolated abstraction when we reason about it. In truth it is intimately related to every circumstance of our daily personal existence. It is the substance, the power, the consciousness expressed in the least of our experiences. It is the source of all our personal light and wisdom, the objective of all our aspirations.

The Hermit is the Supreme Will, the cosmic, eternal urge to freedom. Union with that will is the highest result of the operation of the law that subconsciousness responds to the initiative and suggestions of self–consciousness. Only through the working of the subconscious body–transforming powers can our physical vehicle undergo the subtle changes which make them fit vehicles for union with the Supreme Spirit. This is why Mercury, ruler of Virgo, is also exalted or sublimated in that sign. Mercury is the Magician, the self–training in right interpretation of experience, in concentration, in manipulation of the subconsciousness is what finally bears fruit in union with what is here pictured as the Hermit. In that union the sense of personal *self* is lost, and one knows nothing but the I AM. Hence occult teachings frequently describe the experience as Isolation, exactly what the title of this ninth trump implies.

Psychologically this is the state of being conscious that all volition is universal, rather than personal. It includes firsthand knowledge of the law of the eternal freedom of the true self. This carries with it the perception that the idea of *personal* will, in the sense of a will originating in, or inhering in, personality must be an illusion. This consciousness, *the demonstration of the existence of the primordial glory*, is the true basis of the mighty works of adepts, the foundation of the miracles which are the evidence of genuine sainthood. Thus, and also because it is consciousness of the true basis of all manifestations, the Hermit bears the number which Hebrew occultism associates with *Basis* or *Foundation*. This number, IX, it should be remarked, is also the number which Qabalists ascribe to the reproductive organs of Adam Qadmon, the Archetypal Man. For sages are agreed that although Intelligence of Will seems to be the outcome of personal effort and aspiration, it is really the final stage of a work initiated and carried on by the Life power itself. That work, they say, is one in which the Heavenly Man reproduces himself in the image of the earthly. Herein some may find a key to the doctrine that the Christos is *begotten, not made.*

THE WHEEL OF FORTUNE

K aph (כ, Hard C or K, value 20) means primarily *a curve*, which should be remembered in connection with the fact that a wheel is attributed in the Tarot to this letter. It is the hand of man in the act of grasping. To grasp is to master, to hold, to comprehend. Mentally, what can be grasped is intelligible, clear, explicit, positive, definite, and precise. All these ideas, it will be seen, are in sharp contrast to the ineffability and abstractness of those which are related to Yod and the Hermit.

Wealth and Poverty is the pair of opposites attributed to Kaph. These are the extremes of poverty, external signs of one's grasp of circumstances.

West, place of sunset, symbolizes completion of a cosmic day, of a cycle of manifestation. Even this is in agreement with the symbol of the closed hand, for the day's work closes in the setting of the sun. Completion, accomplishment, mastery, success, and like ideas are all implied. Hence it is written, "Westward the course of empire takes its way," for the facts of history are but the veils of cosmic law. Thus, too, the Occidental world is the world in which practical grasp of material powers is the characteristic mark of success, in contrast to the Orient, where a man's wealth is more likely to be reckoned in terms of his understanding of those

103

laws of mental germination which are typified in the Tarot by the Empress, to whom the direction East is assigned.

Jupiter, the planet attributed to Kaph, rules the zodiacal signs Sagittarius (XIV, Temperance) and Pisces (XVIII, The Moon). Jupiter is also exalted in Cancer (VII, The Chariot, wherein Jupiter's influence is symbolized by the wheels). Jupiter is called *the greater fortune* in contrast to Venus (Empress), who is *the lesser fortune*. In astrology it signifies judges, bankers, theologians – that is, men who have a firm grasp on the lucid, comprehensive statement of ideas, and their application to practical affairs. It is said to govern the circulation of the blood, and circular motion generally. Its color is violet, its musical tone B–flat or A–sharp.

Intelligence of Conciliation, or Rewarding Intelligence of Those Who Seek. Conciliation is the adjustment of differences, the establishment of harmony and order, and thus is distinctly Jovian. The mode of consciousness here indicated is also that which brings perception of the law which fulfills the promise, "Seek, and ye shall find." Conciliation implies concord, agreement, sympathy, peace, amity, and tranquility. The law here shown is that which reconciles apparent differences, which enables us to harmonize the elements of existence, which leads to the winning over of seemingly antagonistic forces, which conduces to peace and prosperity.

The Wheel of Fortune combines the ideas of rotation, cyclicity, sequence, whirling motion, simultaneous descent and ascent (involution and evolution), and so on, with the ideas of fortune, destiny, chance, fate, necessity, probability, and the like. Occult teaching emphatically asserts that what seems to be chance – whether absence of purpose or absence of design – is really the working of unalterable law. The rotation of circumstances appears to be accidental, but is not really so. Every effect is the consequence of preceding causes, and the better we grasp this law of sequence and cyclicity, the greater our command over subsequent events. There is periodicity in everything. The affairs of men and nations have a rhythm, regularity, a steadiness of beat that enables the wise to read the meaning of the present in the history of the past, and forecast the events of the future from close examination of present tendencies. The wheel, moreover, is a symbol of progress, advancement, improvement, and so represents the march of culture, civilization and amelioration which in occultism is called the Great Work.

The design of the tenth major trump in this version of the Tarot is adapted from Eliphas Levi's diagram of the *Wheel of Ezekiel* in his Ritual of the Sanctum Regnum. At the corners of the card, seated on clouds, are the mystical animals mentioned in Ezekiel (i. 10) and Revelation (iv. 7). They correspond to the fixed signs of the zodiac; the Bull to Taurus; the Lion to Leo; the Eagle to Scorpio; the Man to Aquarius. The numbers of these signs are 2, 5, 8 and 11, whose sum is 26, the number of IHVH. In this name, I is represented by the Lion, H by the Eagle, V by the Man, and the final H by the Bull. Thus the *living creatures* typify the fixed, eternal modes of that One Reality that, so to say, remain permanent in the midst of the flux and reflux represented by the turning wheel. That which was, is, and shall be remains ever the same in itself, and the whole sequence and rotation of events goes on within it.

The wheel is the symbol of the whole cycle of cosmic expression, and also the emblem of any particular series of events. Its center, or pivot, is the archetypal world; the inner circle is the creative; the middle circle the formative; the outer circle the material world. The eight spokes are like the eight–pointed star, symbol of universal radiant energy. The creative circle is also the same as the symbol of the Life Breath ten times repeated on the dress of The Fool. On the spokes of the wheel, in the circle representing the formative world, are the alchemical symbols of mercury (above), sulphur (to the right), and salt (to the left). Below is the alchemical symbol of dissolution, identical with the astrological symbol of Aquarius. Sulphur is activity, salt is substance and form, mercury is consciousness. Dissolution is said to be the fundamental process of the Great Work.

A yellow serpent, whose movement suggests vibration, and whose color is that of light, also that assigned to the planet Mercury (I, the Magician) and the sign Leo (VIII, Strength), descends on the left side of the wheel. His descent represents the involution of the cosmic radiant energy into the conditions of name and form. He is the serpent–power (Teth), he is also the energy which descends through the Magician to the garden, and this force bears the message or impulse of the cosmic will.

Hermanubis (Hermes–Anubis), jackal–headed Egyptian god, rises on the right of the wheel, in representation of the evolution of consciousness from lower to higher forms. His jackal's head represents intellectuality. His red color typifies desire and activity. He symbolizes the average level of our present human development of consciousness. Beyond him is a segment of the wheel which only the few, as yet, have traversed.

The sphinx typifies the real Self of man, behind the veil of personality. It is known by the unfoldment of the inner senses corresponding to the outer ones. Then we become aware of the One Thing which transcends personality. That is the propounder of the riddles of existence. It remains motionless while the wheel turns. Its blue color relates it to memory, the characteristic function of the subjective mind, as if to reiterate the idea that the highest self–knowledge is really self–recollection.

On the wheel, in the circle representing the material world, are the letters TARO, counter changed with the Hebrew letters of I H V H, In Hebrew values the letters of TARO make the number 671, important in the Qabalah as the number of certain titles of Malkuth, the Kingdom. As the value of IHVH is 26, the Hebrew values of all the letters on the wheel total 697, whose digits add to 22, number of the circle or wheel, and number of letters in the Hebrew alphabet represented by major trumps in the Tarot.

By transposition, the letters of TARO may be read thus: ROTA TARO ORAT TORA ATOR. This is a somewhat barbarous Latin sentence meaning, *The Wheel of the Tarot speaks the Law of Hathor* (or *The Law of Nature*).

Psychologically, this trump refers to the law of periodicity in mental activity, by which mental states have a tendency to recur in definite rhythms. It is the law, too, of the evolution of undifferentiated conscious energy and its evolution through personalized forms of itself. Finally, it is the law of cause and consequence which enables us to be certain of reaping what we have sown.

JUSTICE

L amed (ל, L, value 30) means, as a verb, *to teach, to instruct*; as a noun, *ox–goad*, that which urges and guides the Ox (Aleph, the Fool).

Work or action is the function assigned to Lamed. Work is the literal meaning of the Sanskrit term Karma.

South–West combines South (XIX, The Sun) with West (X, The Wheel of Fortune). Here is suggested the combination of the cosmic radiance with specific, definite modes of expression resulting from mental grasp of the Law of Cause and Consequence typified by the Wheel. Justice, indeed, is a picture embodying deductions from the ideas represented by the preceding picture. Karma is the subjective working of the cycles of cosmic law.

Libra, the Scales, is a cardinal airy sign. It is ruled by Venus (III, Empress) and is the sign of the exaltation of Saturn (XXI, The World). For our subconscious deductions from experience are the seeds of Karma, and the incentives to work. From them, too, we gain instruction and knowledge. Furthermore, the highest manifestation of the restrictive, concrete, definitive power of Saturn is brought about through the law represented in Justice. Libra governs the kidneys, loins and back. Librans are said by astrologers to love justice, order and harmony.

Their Venusian quality is shown by their love of beauty and culture. They have keen sense of comparison, foresight, and acute perceptions. The Libran color is green. Its musical tone is F–sharp or G–flat.

Faithful Intelligence. The Hebrew for *faithful* is אמן, AMN, Amen, which we say at the end of prayers as a confirmatory expression. It is closely related to the Hindu *Om*, and to the Egyptian god–name AMUN, often written AMEN. In the Hebrew Wisdom it is said that "spiritual virtues are deposited in the Faithful Intelligence, and augment therein." Here is the very idea of the ripening of perception and interpretation into motives for action which is associated with the Sanskrit term Karma.

Justice, the title, signifies the active administration of law. It also makes us think of balance, poise, exactitude, accuracy, impartiality, equity, and the like.

The central figure of the design is a conventional figure of Justice, but she wears no blindfold. The yellow background and purple veil are complementary colors attributed to the element air, ruling the sign Libra. The pillars and veil are similar to those of the High Priestess, whose number, II, is the digit value of XI. The turreted crown with a square jewel conceals the number 7 (three turrets, four sides to the square). This is the Qabalistic number of Venus, whose magic square is 7 by 7. The green cape is of the color occultly attributed to Venus. It is fastened by a brooch composed of square and circle, or 4 and

110

22, representing IHVH. The red robe symbolizes action, attributed to Lamed. The sword has a
T–cross handle, because the T–cross represents
the letter Tau, to which letter is attributed the
planet Saturn, exalted in Libra. Scales are characteristic symbols of Justice and of Libra. The
seat of Justice is cubical, like that of the High
Priestess.

The general meaning is that education (ox–
goad) has equilibration for its aim. It requires,
therefore, the elimination of useless and out-
worn forms (sword, and attribution of Libra
to kidneys). Education is completed by action
and work. Hearing the word, or reading it, is
not education. Action is required, and action is
motivated by subjective response to objective
knowledge.

This card also indicates the truth that subjective mind is the agency whereby the Law
of Cause and Effect (X, The Wheel) is brought
down into the specialized activities of human
life. That in which we have faith determines our
actions, and by our actions we are educated.

Psychologically this picture illustrates the law
of poise and self–direction. The balanced personality is faithful, confident, because right use
of reason has established enduring certainty in
the just outcome of all activities. For the practical occultist this card signifies: (1) You really
know only when you have acted; (2) Equilibration, physical, mental, financial, demands the
elimination of waste, the getting rid of *excess
baggage.*

THE HANGED MAN

Mem (**ם**, M, value 40) is the second of the three mother letters of the Hebrew alphabet. Its name means literally *seas* or *ocean*. Thus it is the letter of water, which alchemists called *mother, seed, and root of all minerals.*

In ancient books neither direction nor planet is assigned to this letter. In modern astrology, however, Neptune corresponds to Mem. The color of this planet is pale blue, and its musical tone is G–sharp or A–flat.

Water is the element assigned to Mem. Water is the first mirror. Thus it is the symbol of reflected life, of life in image, of life in the forms taken by substance.

Hanged Man means occultly, *suspended mind*, because *man* and *mind* are from the same Sanskrit root, and occult schools have always known this fact. The title also refers to the dependence of personality upon the cosmic life.

The T–cross from which the youth hangs is a cross of living wood. It represents the cosmic life. It also represents the letter Tau, which is symbolized in the Tarot by the trump called The World. Then, too, a T–cross is like a T–square, and suggests measurement. Combining these ideas, we get the thought that the reflected life, depending from the cosmic life, depends also upon that measurement of its own powers that characterizes the self–expression of the universal Being. See in this connection the explanation of the number 4, in relation to *Measuring Intelligence.*

In 1918 I received from an occult correspondent the following explanation of the Hanged Man:

> The correct geometrical figure concealed by the Hanged Man is the cross, surmounting a water triangle. It signifies the multiplication of the tetrad by the triad. This is the number 12. The *door*, Daleth, is the vehicle of the tetrad, for it is the Great Womb also; and the head of the Hanged Man reflected therein is the LVX, in manifestation as the Logos. He is Osiris, Sacrifice, and Yod–Heh–Shin–Vau–Heh, Yehoshua.

This is explanation enough for an advanced occultist, but requires some elaboration for the purposes of this book. It is evident that the legs of the Hanged Man form a cross and that lines drawn from his elbows to the point formed by his hair will form the sides of a reversed triangle having his arms for its base.

The cross is the number 4, and the triangle is the number 3. The multiplication of these two numbers gives 12, which, because it is the number of signs in the zodiac, represents a complete cycle of manifestation.

The inverted triangle is, among other things, one of the ancient ways of writing the letter

Daleth, which corresponds to the Empress, numbered 3 in the Tarot. She is what the Hindus call Prakriti, the Great Womb of cosmic substance, the generatrix of all forms. By a similar numeral correspondence, the crossed legs of the Hanged Man may be taken to represent the Emperor, since they indicate the number 4. Thus they are red, the color of fire, representing action, and also the particular quality of the sign Aries, which the Emperor typifies.

The upper garment of the Hanged Man is blue, color of Water, of the robe of the High Priestess, and symbol of mind stuff. Water, too, is represented by the inverted triangle in alchemical symbolism.

The head of the Hanged Man ... is LVX, in manifestation as the Logos, means that his head, by its white hair, suggests identity with the Hermit and the Emperor. He is the Ancient of Days, reflected into the incarnate life of personality. One of the old occult names for the One Life is LVX, which is Latin for *Light*, but which also is an occult reference to the Hebrew name *Adonai*, or *Lord*. For the numeral values of the letters L, V and X are respectively 50, 5 and 10, whose sum is 65, and 65 is the numeration of the Hebrew name אדני, ADNI, Adonai. The One Light is the Word which is made flesh, and is then represented by the esoteric Hebrew spelling of the name Jesus, that is, יהשוה, IHShVH Yod–Heh–Shin–Vau–Heh, Yehoshua.

These, however, are meanings of the picture that will not be likely to seem as important as they really are until the student has made considerable advance along the occult path. Fortunately, there are other meanings, less withdrawn from ordinary ways of thinking, but by no means less important. To these I shall devote the rest of this section.

Here is a man turned upside down, inverted, in a position contrary to that in which we find most people. Tradition says, by the way, that St. Peter was crucified in this position, and the tradition may have more than a hint for us, when combined with the idea that Peter is the *rock of foundation*. For the very basis of the occult approach to life, the foundation of the everyday practice of the person who lives the life of obedience to esoteric law, is the reversal of the more usual ways of thinking, speaking and doing. Hence Boehme says, you will remember that the great secret is "to walk in all things contrary to the world."

The same idea is hinted at in the very garments of the Hanged Man. His legs are red, color of fire, and his body is blue, color of water. These elements are as opposite as light and darkness, as contrary as black and white. Thus opposition is plainly symbolized by the clothes, as well as by the position of the figure.

This does not mean outspoken antagonism to other people. On the contrary, such a spirit is precisely the way of the world which occultists endeavor to avoid. Hence this picture is associated with the letter Mem, of which Qabalists say, "Mem is mute, like water." Silent, unostentatious reversal of one's own way of life, combined with perfect tolerance of the ways of other people, is the method of the practical occultist.

In what, then, does the reversal consist? Primarily in a reversal of thought, in a point of view that is just the opposite of that accepted by most people. At first there may seem to be no practical advantage in this, but just consider. One need only look about him to see that most people are sick, that most people are in trouble, that most people cannot get along with themselves and the world. Does it not become evident, then, that most people are in trouble because they have somehow put the cart before the horse in their practice of life? In this scientific age, we know that everything is an expression of the Law of Cause and Effect. Is it not plain, therefore, that the miseries afflicting most people are the result of their negative use of the law? For every moment of a human life is a special application of the law and the outcome depends wholly upon whether the application is positive or negative.

Practical psychology shows us the potency of ideas. It demonstrates conclusively the truth that thoughts are the seeds of speech and action, that interpretations are the patterns for experience, that what happens to us is what we have selected, whether the selection is conscious and intentional, or unconscious and unpremeditated. Thus in practical psychology the emphasis is upon a changed viewpoint, and the change is no less than a total reversal.

All the ideas that have been considered in our study of the preceding major trump point to the Hanged Man. Here the central thought is that every human being is absolutely dependent upon the All (the tree) for personal existence. As soon as this truth is realized, the only logical and sensible course of conduct is a complete self–surrender. That surrender begins in the mind. It is the surrender of the personal consciousness to the direction of the Universal Mind, and that surrender is foreshadowed even in the picture of the Magician, who clearly derives all his power from above. Until we know that of ourselves we can do nothing, we shall never attain to adeptship. The greater the adept, the more complete is his personal self–surrender.

Paradoxically, this total submission of the personal life to Life Itself makes us intensely positive in relation to other people and in relation to the conditions of our environment. Nobody who follows this course ever becomes a human doormat. For positive mental attitudes require the consciousness of support transcending mere personal human power. In the face of some of the appearances that are bound to confront us as we go through life, we need something more than just our *own* personal energies to carry us through. In order to have courage and persistence in the face of seeming disappointment and difficulty, we must know ourselves as vehicles of a power to which nothing can be an insurmountable obstacle.

The mental attitude suggested by the Hanged

Man, then, is *Not my will, but thine.* This is ever the position of the adept, as, indeed, it is the position of the practical scientist in the fields of physics and chemistry. It is an attitude born of the knowledge that *my will* is an illusory, personal thing that is but the reflection, or the mask, of *Thy Will*, the real Will, which is the purpose or motive of the cosmic Life – a Will absolutely free, and certain to be realized.

This thought does not imply that the Universal Will visits poverty, affliction and disease upon us. It does not mean that we must be resigned to our troubles, like dumb beasts making no complaint when they are beaten. It means that in spite of appearances the cosmic Will works always toward good, that the universal Will–to–good cannot possibly be defeated. It means that personality is known for what it is, a partial expression of the All, and that in consequence our personal notions of what is best for us may often be mistaken. Our notions of the ways in which good is coming to us frequently fall short of what is really headed in our direction. And so long as we continue to make false interpretations, the inexorable laws of the cosmos work out those interpretations in pain–bringing forms.

But pain itself is friendly, because it is educative. Suffering, poverty, disease, disharmony and death are in reality educative influences. These are the things that prod the race onward in its search for truth. I do not pretend to understand why this is the method, although sometimes it seems to me that the very fact of existence implies temporary limitation, with suffering as an inevitable consequence of that limitation. But one does not need to be a philosopher to know that civilization is the fruit of human reaction against pain, of human quest for ways to overcome limitation. Disease teaches us the laws of health, disharmony goads us into the discovery of the secret of harmony, and the wise declare that in the mystery of death is hidden the secret of immortality.

Such thoughts as these are the exact reverse of what most people think. Such practices in mind–control and body–direction as are suggested by psychologists and occultists are laughed at by the world, and people who take them seriously are popularly regarded as men upside–down. Yet the world's ridicule should be the best evidence that the occultists are right. For the world is sick unto death, groaning in pain, ridden by war and pestilence and famine. But the wise have found the way of health, of happiness and peace.

DEATH

Nun (נ, N, value 50) is pronounced *noon* and as a noun means *fish*. As a verb, because fish are extraordinarily prolific, it means *to sprout, to grow*. The essential idea is fertility, fecundity, productiveness, generative power, and these ideas are bound up in thought and language with such words as cause, origin, source, mainspring, groundwork, leaven, and the like.

Motion is the function attributed to Nun by Qabalists, and the Hebrew word for it has the primary meaning *to walk*. From this are derived a great variety of other meanings such as to travel, to grow, to depart, to pass away, to whirl, to sail away, and so on. All motion is change, transformation, variation, modification. Thus, by linking up these ideas with the thought of foundation or groundwork implied by the meanings of the letter Nun, we get the conception that change is the basis of manifestation.

North–West combines North (XVI, The Tower), which is a picture of violent change, and refers to the planet Mars, with West (X, The Wheel), which represents the revolution or whirling of the cosmic Life Breath through the various forms of manifestation. West also relates to the planet Jupiter, which governs all rotation and circular movement. For the permutations and transformations in this world of name and form are all in cycles.

Scorpio, the Scorpion, is a fixed watery sign. It is ruled by Mars (XVI, The Tower), and is said by modern astrologers to be the sign of the exaltation of Uranus (O, The Fool). This sign governs the sex organs, and is therefore closely associated in astrology with reproduction. It is, moreover, connected with the eighth *house* of the horoscope, which is called the house of death, and thus Scorpio is plainly indicated by the title of the thirteenth major trump. The corresponding color is greenish–blue. The musical tone is G–natural.

Imaginative Intelligence is the mode of consciousness. Qabalists say, "It is the ground of similarity in the likeness of beings." That is, it is the basis of the resemblances which are transmitted through the reproductive functions. The choice of the term *Imaginative* is in accordance with the conception of the Ageless Wisdom that causation is mental. Hence all changes are primarily changes in mental imagery. Change the image and ultimately the external form will change.

Death, the title, obviously relates to the astrological meaning of Nun. Death, the Bible, says, is the last enemy to be overcome. But how? "Overcome evil with good. Love your enemies." In these two brief sentences is the whole secret. The forces of change which result in physical death are inimical only because we misunderstand and fear them. They are forces connected with reproduction, and by right use of imagination may be tamed and transformed, so that they can be utilized for the indefinite prolongation of physical existence. Death, like every other event in human life, is a manifestation of law. Understanding of the forces expressed through that law enables us to control them. But understanding will never be ours until fear, not only of dying, but of death itself, has been overcome by right knowledge and right interpretations.

The symbolism in the Rider pack is Mr. Waite's personal variation from the older versions. The latter shows a skeleton with a scythe, in a field where there are living hands, feet and heads protruding from the ground. These are being reaped by the skeleton.

The present version is better symbolism, because it plainly intimates that death is a friend in the guise of a foe. It also has special reference to certain changes peculiar to the present era of history.

Sunrise in the background suggests dawn, and as dawn is pictured in the Tarot by the Fool, this may be taken to suggest the influence of the planet Uranus. This planet is said to be exalted in Scorpio, and since Uranus governs all things occult, it is undoubtedly responsible for the revival of interest in the sciences during this present era. Those sciences, moreover, on their practical side lead sooner or later to knowledge of the hidden law of life veiled in the mystery of death.

In general the landscape in the middle distance is like that in the background of the fourth major trump, the Emperor. One sees the same high bluffs, with a river at their base. The river is the stream of consciousness. On it floats a boat, with sail set to a strong breeze blowing from the North. (North, remember, is the direction corresponding to the planet Mars.) The river and the boat move southward, toward the place of the sun's meridian height, that is, toward the place related to the zenith, or highest point of manifestation. The rider journeys in the same direction, which is attributed in the Tarot to the Sun, and to the nineteenth major trump.

The rider is a skeleton, clad in black armor. The armor signifies Mars, and its color denotes occult or hidden phases of the Mars activity. The skeleton is the basis, or essential thing, in all movements of the human body. Similarly, change or transformation – particularly the transformation connected with reproduction – is the skeleton which supports the whole body of phenomenal existence. Thus Mr. Waite says, "The veil or mask of life is perpetuated in change, transformation and passage from lower to higher." The horse is the *pale horse* mentioned in Revelation. In this picture it is white, but the word *chloros*, translated *pale* in the English Bible means literally, *greenish*, which corresponds not only to the sign Scorpio, but also suggests the idea of growth associated with Nun. Any horse is a symbol of solar energy.

The banner carried by the skeleton rider is a white rose on a square black ground. The petals and sepals of the rose number 15, the number of trefoils on the crown of the Hierophant. It is a white rose like that borne by the Fool, and signifies the purification of the desire nature. The black square means measurement (square) of the occult (black) forces. Thus the standard combines the idea of the measurement of occult forces with that of the purification of desire. The particular hidden forces indicated are those which are connected with the functions that are governed by the sign Scorpio. To measure and master them is to overcome death, for in the operation of those forces is concealed the law of regenerative change. Methods of mastery are not taught in books or lectures; but it may be said that the regenerative change is a sublimation and redirection of nervous energies (not fluids or secretions). This redirection of nerve forces is effected by exercises in special kinds of creative imagination. When you, the reader of this page, are duly and truly prepared for further instruction, nothing can prevent you from receiving it. Part of your preparation, and part of the testing process by which your readiness is determined, is your study of the Tarot. You have not come into touch with it by chance. Every event in your life is an expression of law, and your acquaintance with the picture book of Ageless Wisdom has come about through the working of a law whereby the Inner School tries the fitness of every promising candidate for genuine initiation and advancement.

Before the advancing rider a king lies dead,

signifying the passing away of the monarchical idea of government. A child and woman kneel, representing the passing away (not yet completed) of the old, harsh, barbarous notions of the place of woman and children in society. A priest, wearing a fish head miter (emblem of the Piscean religious dispensation) awaits his end, to show that as we pass into the Aquarian Age, the forms of religion developed during the Piscean Age must give place to others better suited to the needs of humanity in the new dispensation.

It is by death that these social changes came about. Old ideas pass away with the death of the people who hold them. New ideas gain currency as the new generation come to maturity. Thus the actual fact of death is an instrument of progress. And now the time is at hand when we shall master the secret of death itself.

Psychologically, the emphasis falls on imagination. Change your ideas and the old conception of personality dies. Every few years you have a new body, made up of trillions of tiny beings, or cells. Change your intellectual patterns, and with the passing away of the present generation of cells new ones will come to take their places. And in the mental nucleus of each tiny cell, implanted there by the subconscious response to your new patterns, will be the impulse to realize the new thought in body–structure, in function, and in external action.

If your pattern is built in accordance with the ideas developed through the Tarot series and culminating in the self–surrender pictured by the Hanged Man, it will lead to a complete transformation of your personality. The *old man* dies. One who arrives at this state can say with St. Paul, "I die daily." Every morning becomes a resurrection to the awakened soul. All the old motives, all the petty ambitions, all the foolish opinions and prejudices gradually die out, as the cells which carry them are eliminated in the ordinary course of body repair. Thus, little by little, there comes a complete readjustment of all one's personal conceptions of life and its values. This change from the personal to the universal viewpoint is so radical that mystics often compare it to death. Moreover, they are more literal than many of their readers suppose. It is by the death and reproduction of body–cells that the patterns created by imagination are finally fixed in personal consciousness. Then it is that we may truly declare, "The Kingdom of Spirit is embodied in my flesh."

TEMPERANCE

amekh (ם, soft C, S, value 60) means *tent–peg*, or *prop*. It is what makes a tent secure, and thus corresponds to what would now be suggested to us by the foundation of a house. It is therefore the letter symbol of that which is the basis or support of our house of life. It is that which sustains, preserves and maintains our personal existence.

Wrath is the quality associated with Samekh, but this is a *blind*. The literal meaning of the original Hebrew word is *quivering* or *vibration*. A similar *blind* is found in the use of the Greek noun thumos, also translated *wrath* in the New Testament. The Hebrew word is רוגז, RVGZ, and its number is 216, equivalent to ראיה, RAIH, sight, the function attributed to the Emperor; to אריה, ARIH, Arieh, the Lion, name of the sign associated with the Tarot picture of Strength; and to גבורה, GBVRH, Geburah, Severity, the name of the strength aspect of the number 5. The numerical correspondence between these Hebrew words indicates a basic identity of meaning. Vibration is the basic nature of the fiery power which makes sight possible, and that same power is the source of all our strength. Furthermore, when translated into Tarot pictures, the word רוגז, RVGZ becomes the sequence: The Sun – The Hierophant – The High Priestess – The Lovers. Lay out this series of pictures on a table and study them. You will get intimations as to the real meaning of the vibratory force that would otherwise escape you. Note also that the first letter corresponds to the sun, the second to the sign Taurus ruled by Venus, the third to the Moon, and the last to Gemini ruled by Mercury. Finally, add the numbers of the Tarot trumps. The result is 32. As there is no major trump bearing this number, add the digits, and the result, 5, is the number of the Hierophant. This, too, is the number resulting from the reduction of 14, the number of Temperance.

The idea is that vibration is the basis of manifestation, and that essentially all vibration is like sound, the mode of vibration particularly associated with the Hierophant. Vibration is fluctuating motion, undulation, pulsation, alternation. It takes wave forms.

West–Above, the direction assigned to Samekh, combines West (X, The Wheel) with Above (I, the Magician). Here is indicated the combination of the idea of cycles and rotation with that of concentration and attentive observation of experience. We shall find this developed in the picture of Temperance.

Sagittarius, the Archer, is a fiery common sign, ruled by Jupiter (X, The Wheel of Fortune). It governs the thighs and hips, which support the weight of the body in standing and sitting. Its color correspondence is blue, its musical tone G–sharp or A–flat.

Tentative Intelligence, or Intelligence of Probation, indicates a mode of consciousness wherein experience becomes the test of ideas. It is the kind of consciousness which puts theory to the test of practical application, which makes experiments to verify hypotheses, which does laboratory work. All that work consists in the examination and modification of various modes of vibration.

Temperance, in the days when the Tarot was invented meant *tempering* or *modifying*. It therefore suggests adaptation. (Here note that the digit value of XIV is V, and 5 means adaptation.) Adaptation is the basis of all practical work in Hermetic science. The Emerald Tablet says, "As all things are from One, so all have their birth from this One Thing by adaptation." Hermetic scientists endeavor to imitate nature, and adaptation is their method. To adapt is to equalize, to adjust, to coordinate, and to equilibrate. Therefore it is written, "Equilibrium is the basis of the Great Work."

The crown in the background signifies attainment, mastery, and like ideas. It has also a technical reference to the esoteric meanings of the number 1, which Hebrew Wisdom calls *The Crown*. The end of the path of attainment is the realization of the crown of perfect union with the true Unity, or Primal Will. The twin peaks on either side of the Crown are Wisdom (2) and Understanding (3).

The path rising from the pool appears again in the XVIIIth major trump, and will be more fully explained in connection with that card. But here I wish to point out the fact that it rises over rolling ground, and thus imitates the wave-motion which is characteristic in all forms of vibration.

The angel is Michael, angel of the sun, archangel of fire, and ruler of the South (XIX, The Sun). The solar symbol on his head establishes his identity, as does his yellow hair, and the rays streaming from it. The fact that Sagittarius is a fiery sign carries the correspondence still further. So do the fiery wings of the angel.

His white robe represents purity and wisdom. At the neck are written Hebrew letters spelling the name IHVH. Below the letters is a flame-colored upright triangle representing fire and spirit enclosed in a white square representing purified matter. The square and triangle are also similar to the Masonic apron, are the geometrical elements of the Great Pyramid, and symbolize the number 7.

One foot rests on water, symbol of the cosmic mind stuff, the other on land, symbol of concrete material manifestation.

He pours water from the cup in his right hand to that in his left. The cups are of gold to symbolize the idea that all forms of life-expression have radiant energy as their basic substance. The upper cup is self-consciousness, corresponding to the Man in the Lovers. The other is subconsciousness, corresponding to the Woman in the same picture. The stream of water (mind stuff) vibrates between them. Furthermore, action and reaction are intimated, for when the lower cup is filled he will reverse the position of the cups, and that which is now below will become that which is above.

The irises growing behind him are symbols of the Greek goddess Iris, who personifies the rainbow. The rainbow is related to Sagittarius because it is the *Bow of Promise* wherewith the Archer shoots. Recondite Qabalistic meanings are behind this symbolism which it would be unprofitable to enlarge upon here. I have given you a signpost. If you wish to go farther, consider its meaning. Also, look up Iris in a good dictionary of mythology. In this connection it may be mentioned that vases are symbols of Iris, and that in some old Tarots the angel is distinctly feminine.

The angel is the real I AM, adapting and modifying the personal stream of psychic energy in the actions and reactions of the self–conscious and subconscious minds. The practical import of the picture is this: We do nothing of ourselves. The Holy Guardian Angel makes all the tests and trials which lead us along the path of attainment. Know this, but act as if you were making the tests yourself. The only correction necessary is the intellectual correction. For practical purposes, the wise man acts just as if he were doing things *on his own*. He knows better, that's all.

In your practice, shoot at some definite mark. Quit accepting theories and statements – no matter how plausible they sound – until you have tested them out in actual practice. The purpose of the Ageless Wisdom is to get you to try,

133

not to persuade you to accept. Thus it is written, "The only failure is the failure to try." By trial you will soon realize that the real working power which makes the experiments is something higher than your personality. It is the Angel on whose robe is written the identifying name of That which was, and is and shall be.

Finally, all your experiments will be in equalization, in the co–ordination of vibratory activities. There is nothing in the cosmos but vibration, and all forms of vibration, may be modified and managed by mental control.

THE DEVIL

Ayin ($\mathbf{y}$, O, value 70) means *eye* and *fountain*. As organ of sight, the eye is the most important sense tool; hence symbolists take it to represent all sensation, just as the lion, king of beasts, is taken as the representative of all subhuman modes of Life–expression. The eye is an orb; vision is limited by the circle of the horizon; through the eye we see only appearance; hence, subtly, the eye represents the limitations of the visible, and the bondage of ignorance resulting from accepting these limitations and appearances as being all there is.

Mirth, the function of consciousness attributed to Ayin, is usually caused by incongruity, by human weaknesses and shortcomings. Nevertheless, laughter is prophylactic. It purifies subconsciousness and dissolves mental conflicts. In a hymn to the sun god Ra, we read: "Thy priests go forth at dawn, they wash their hearts with laughter." This is a prescription we may all follow to advantage.

West–Below combines West (X, The Wheel) with Below (II, The High Priestess). Here is an intimation that whatever is denoted by the Devil in the Tarot is the result of the impression made by the apparent mechanical, fatal revolutions of circumstance (The Wheel) upon the subjective mind (High Priestess).

Capricorn, the Goat, is a cardinal, earthly sign,

governing the knees, to which we are brought in prayer by our sense of bondage and personal insufficiency. The natives of Capricorn are quiet, studious, but rather inclined to be materialistic. Saturn (XXI, The World) rules Capricorn, and Mars (XVI, The Tower) is exalted therein. Its color correspondence is blue–violet, its musical tone A–natural.

Renewing Intelligence is the mode of consciousness attributed to Ayin. This is directly related to Mirth, because the perception of incongruities is what actually brings forth new ideas and adaptations. An incongruity is something that does not fit. When we find a fact that does not fit in with our beliefs, we are obliged to revise our theories, unless we are the sort of *green apple* that prefers a comfortable lie to an uncomfortable truth.

It has been, indeed, the incongruity between man's apparent bondage to circumstance and his ineradicable intuition that somehow or other he is intended to rule nature which has driven the race forward in those avenues of research which lead to freedom.

Internally, we know that we are potential lords of creation. But here we meet a check, and there a defeat, and so we try to explain why we are not actually as free as we feel ourselves internally to be. The symbolism of the picture ascribed to Ayin represents the cruder forms of man's answers to this question, and at the same time subtly indicates the correct solution, and the way out of the difficulty.

The Devil is the English for Latin *diabolus*, adversary. The picture refers to man's ideas of the nature of that which seems so relentlessly to oppose his struggles for freedom. In commenting on this, I wish once more to remind you of the words ascribed to Jehovah in Isaiah 45. Remember, too, that the Devil personifies the serpent–power represented by Teth and Strength. The name for the serpent which tempted Eve is נחש, NChSh, Nachash, numerically equivalent to משיח, MShICH, Messiah. Here is a profound subtlety, for numerical identity between Hebrew words points to some inner correspondence of meaning. Finally, it has been said, "The Devil is God as He is misunderstood by the wicked."

The number of this trump is 15, which is the number of יה, IH, Jah, a divine name especially ascribed to Wisdom. The same number is shown by the petals and sepals of the rose on Death's banner, and by the number of trefoils on the crown of the Hierophant. 15, by addition of digits, is reducible to 6, the number of the Lovers. Furthermore, 15 is the sum of the numbers from 1 to 5, so that the Hierophant (5), regarded as the summation of a series beginning with 1, also refers to 15. Compare, now, the Devil with the lovers and the Hierophant.

The background is black, color of ignorance, darkness, limitation, and also of that which is occult or hidden. Here is an intimation that the underlying cause of bondage is ignorance. Also a hint that the ridiculous figure of the Devil is

a veil for a profound secret of practical occultism.

The Devil himself is the polar opposite of the
angel shown in the preceding major trump. He
is also a caricature of the angel over the heads
of the Lovers, even as the figures below him are
bestialized reproductions of the man and woman in the sixth trump.

Goat's horns on his head refer to the sign
Capricorn. His wings are bat's wings, signifying
powers of darkness. His face is that of a don-
key, to suggest the obstinacy and stubbornness
of materialism. His body is thickset and gross,
to represent the earthy quality of the sign Capricorn.

Over his head is a Pentagram, but ill-propor-
tioned and reversed. This, in a sense, is the key
to the whole meaning of the figure. For the Pentagram is the symbol of Man, and an ill-drawn,
reversed Pentagram suggests the reversal of the
true measurement and understanding of man's
place in the cosmos. Its false proportions indicate maladjustment. In point of fact, this is all
that keeps any one in bondage – this mistaken
estimate of man's powers and possibilities.

His uplifted right hand has all the fingers open,
as if in contradiction of the sign of esotericism
made by the Hierophant. The latter's gesture
says, *What you see is not all there is to know.*
The Devil's gesture intimates, *What sensation
reports is all there is to it.* On the palm of this
uplifted hand is outlined an astrological symbol
of the planet Saturn, ruling in Capricorn. Saturn

is the planet of limitation, inertia, and therefore of ignorance.

In his left hand is a torch, held wrong side up, so that it burns wastefully and gives little light. The torch is a phallic symbol, representing the transmission of life from generation to generation, and it is also a symbol of enlightenment. Its fiery quality refers also to the exaltation of the Mars vibration (XVI, The Tower) in Capricorn. In one sense this is the fiery torch of revolution, based upon materialistic interpretations of experience, the torch of terrorism and anarchy.

It may be worth mentioning that the Devil here pictured has a navel. He is a human product, begotten of man's ignorance. Sometimes a symbol of Mercury is shown on this part of his body, to indicate that he is the product of faulty observation and superficial reasoning.

His feet are the claws of the Eagle. The Eagle is the bird corresponding to the sign Scorpio. Here the eagle's claws refer to the materialization and misuse of the reproductive energies, and to their debasement in the service of sensuality.

The Devil sits on a pedestal which is a half–cube. Since a cube represents That which was, is and shall be, the half cube represents half–knowledge of that reality. Half–knowledge perceives nothing but the visible, sensory side of existence. To this half–cube are chained the smaller figures, representing self–conscious and subconscious modes of human mentality. Their horns, hoofs and tails show that when reasoning takes its premises from surface appearances, human consciousness becomes bestialized.

This picture represents the first stage of spiritual unfoldment. It is the stage of conscious bondage. The devil personifies the false conception that man is bound by material conditions, the false notion that he is a slave to necessity, or the sport of chance. In truth, the forces that appear to be our adversaries are always ready to serve us. The one condition is that we understand our essential freedom, and take account of the hidden side of existence. Then, when we conform our practice to our knowledge, progressive liberation begins. The Devil is sensation, divorced by ignorance from understanding. Yet he is also what brings renewal, because we can make no real effort to be free until we feel our limitations. Until our chains irk us, we can make no efforts to strike them off.

THE TOWER

Peh (ⴖ, P, Ph, F, value 80) means *the mouth as the organ of speech.* It therefore symbolizes power of utterance. Out of it are the issues of life.

North is the place of darkness, of the unknown, of the sun's annual death. It is the opposite of South (XIX, The Sun).

Mars, the planet attributed to Peh, rules Aries (IV, The Emperor) and Scorpio (XIII, Death), and is exalted in Capricorn (XV, The Devil). The Mars vibration is scientific, and is active in sight. It is also active in reproduction, and is the iconoclastic, destructive force that tears down the structure of ancient custom and tradition. It is also the fiery power of action regnant in the human body. Its color is scarlet, its musical tone C–natural.

Grace and Sin, or Beauty and Ugliness, are the pair of opposites attributed to the letter Peh, because the issues of life, directed by human speech, result in one or the other. Sin, or *missing the mark*, results in maladjustment and ugliness. Hitting the mark results in the manifestation of beauty.

Exciting Intelligence is clearly the mode of consciousness which stirs up activity, sets things going, produces changes, and so on.

The Tower refers traditionally to the Tower of Babel, at which human speech was confounded. Sometimes this trump is called *The House of God*, as indicating the exoteric theological structure of religious belief. Note that the number of the card is 16, which digits to 7, the card attributed to Speech.

The lightning is a male symbol. In the Bhagavad–Gita, Krishna says: "Among weapons, I am the thunderbolt." It is interesting to note that a scientist in the Westinghouse laboratories has recently photographed artificial lightning flashes, with the result that they are shown to be spirals, instead of zigzags. This fact may have been known to the ancients, for the Chaldean Oracles of Zoroaster speak of the Supreme Spirit as *the god who energizes a spiral force*. Among the ancients, lightning was an emblem of fecundation and nutrition, as well as of destruction. Plutarch says, "The agriculturalists call the lightning the fertilizer of the waters and so regard it."

The lightning flash is the power drawn from above by the Magician; the sword of the Charioteer; the sceptre of the Emperor; the force which turns the Wheel of Fortune; the scythe of Death. It breaks down existing forms in order to make room for new ones. It is also a symbol of the tenfold emanation of the Life power, for the Book of Formation says: "Ten ineffable numerations; their appearance is like that of a flash of lightning, their goal is infinite." In terms of consciousness, the lightning flash symbolizes a sudden, momentary glimpse of truth, a flash of inspiration which breaks down structures of ignorance and false reasoning.

The tower is the garden of the Magician, the throne of the Emperor, the Chariot, the turning Wheel, the figures which fall before Death. It is subconsciousness, considered as the root substance which takes form, first as mental images, and ultimately as physical things. From moment to moment, throughout all time, it is being transformed. It is the *Prakriti* of the Hindus, concerning which it is written: "True knowledge makes Prakriti disappear, first as containing Purusha (the I AM), and then as separate from Purusha."

The falling figures correspond to the chained figures of the preceding picture. They fall head-first, because the sudden influx of spiritual consciousness represented by the lightning flash completely upsets all our old notions about the relations between subconsciousness and self–consciousness.

These are clothed figures, and the man wears both red and blue, to show a mixture of conscious and subjective activities. Similarly, the woman is shod with red, but wears a blue robe. The woman, furthermore, is crowned. In false knowledge, the subjective motives are allowed to dominate the personality. Thus people excuse themselves for unintelligent action by saying, *I can't help it. That's the way I feel.* This dominance of personality by emotion, and by telepathic invasion through the activity of the subjective mind, is overcome by right knowledge. So, too, is the concealment and division between consciousness and subconsciousness, here indicated by the fact that the falling figures are fully clothed.

The crown knocked from the tower by the lightning flash is the materialistic notion that matter and form are the ruling principles of existence. Since *Crown* is a technical Qabalistic term relating to the number 1, and to Will, this Crown also refers to the false monism of the materialist, and to the false interpretation of will which makes it something personal, something that can be set against the impulse originating in the cosmic Purpose.

Twenty–two Hebrew Yods are shown, ten on one side of the tower, and twelve on the other side. They represent the twenty–two letters of the Hebrew alphabet, and the forces corresponding thereto. Ten symbolize the elementary and planetary letters. Twelve represent the zodiacal letters.

This picture corresponds to the second stage of spiritual unfoldment, wherein a series of sudden, fitful inspirations leads to the perception that the structure of knowledge built on the foundation of personal separation is a tower of false science. At this stage the advancing seeker for freedom suffers the destruction of his whole former philosophy. For this tower is built upon a foundation of misapprehension, and the whole structure is a subjective elaboration of superficial observation, traditional race thought, false reasoning and an erroneous theory of will.

THE STAR

Tzaddi (ℵ, Ts, Tz, or Cz as in *Czar*, value 90) means fish–hook, signifying that which draws the fish (Nun) out of the Water (Mem). The water is reflected, personal existence, symbolized by the Hanged Man. It is also, in a sense, the ocean of subconscious mentality. The fish symbolizes transforming and reproductive power. The activity which lifts the fish up out of the material relations of personal existence, and utilizes the reproductive forces as a regenerative agency, is here indicated.

Now, the fish–hook is the symbol of angling. Thus, in our thought it is related to the ideas of experimentation, quest, and research. It is a quest for that which is not definitely realized as yet, a sort of groping, a feeling of one's way that we speak of as *fishing*. What is clearly intimated here is that whatever the fish–hook symbolizes must be some agency or instrumentality whereby one investigates the unseen and the unknown, whereby one makes attempts to solve secrets or enigmas, whereby one follows a more or less faint trail leading to the solution of a mystery.

Meditation is the function attributed to Tzaddi. It has been defined as *an unbroken flow of knowledge in a particular object.* It is fishing for truth in the depths of the subconsciousness. The Hebrew word means literally *conception,* and is transference to things mental of the idea of physical conception, of the budding or germination of ideas. Conception is mysterious. Germinal processes in both plant and animal organisms go on in darkness. They are, moreover, rudimentary. What we are considering here, therefore, has to do with the first stages of mental unfoldment, with the genesis of ideas rather than with their full development.

Practically, meditation is the only safe regenerative method, because it draws up nerve force from the reproductive centers without any actual fixation of attention upon sex functions.

South–Above combines South (XIX, The Sun) with above (I, The Magician). This is the combination of the radiant energy of the sun with the directive influence of Mercury. In other words, meditation is the direction of the currents of solar force by acts of self–conscious attention.

Aquarius, the Water–bearer, is an airy fixed sign. It is represented by the Man among the *living creatures* of Ezekiel and the Apocalypse. Its astrological symbol is shown on the Wheel of Fortune – two wavy lines, one above the other. This is also the alchemical symbol of dissolution, and we have already seen that solution is one of the ideas connected with the symbol of the fish–hook. The Aquarius symbol, moreover, is one of many Hermetic representations of the axiom, "That which is above is as that which is below." Ancient astrology made Saturn (XII, The World) ruler of this sign. Modern astrologers find that it also receives the influences of

Uranus (O, The Fool). Aquarius governs the ankles. Aquarians are said to be intuitive and fond of occult research. They succeed in pursuits where steady mental application and intense concentration are necessary. That is, they are naturally meditative, naturally given to the pursuit of elusive, difficult modes of truth. All this agrees with the ideas associated with Tzaddi. The color correspondence of Aquarius is violet, its musical tone A–sharp or B–flat.

Natural Intelligence. The Hebrew of the word translated *natural* is from the root תבע, TBO, meaning literally *to sink.* The connection with *fish–hoo*k, which must be dropped in water to catch the fish, is evident. Natural Intelligence, or awareness of the hidden qualities of nature, is arrived at by meditation. This is the great secret of occult power as developed by Oriental adepts. See Patanjali's Yoga Aphorisms, in which are enumerated many *powers* which may be developed by intense concentration.

Because the number XVII reduces to VIII, this picture has occult correspondence to the trump entitled Strength. It shows the method whereby knowledge of the Great Secret is attained. This method solves the mysteries of nature and, as the picture shows, unveils her to the enlightened seer.

The great yellow star signifies the cosmic radiant energy which is collected in the various suns and fixed stars of the universe. It has eight points, like the star on the crown of the Charioteer, and it is also like the eight–spoked Wheel of Fortune. Thus it is likewise a variant of the symbol of Spirit embroidered on the dress of the Fool. This is the solar energy hinted at by the attribution of the direction South–Above to the letter Tzaddi. The makers of the Tarot are always reminding us that in our mental and magical work we are using an actual force which has definite physical forms of expression. Meditation modifies and transmutes the personal expression of this cosmic energy, and that personal expression is what we term nerve force.

The seven smaller stars refer to the seven *interior stars*, which are the same as the *chakras* mentioned by Hindu occultists. They are also the metals of alchemy, and the planets of esoteric astrology. They are: Sacral plexus, Saturn, Lead, *Muladhara chakra*; Prostatic ganglion (below the navel), Mars, Iron, *Svadisthana chakra*; Solar Plexus, Jupiter, Tin, *Manipura chakra*; Cardiac plexus, Sun, Gold, *Anahata chakra*; Pharyngeal plexus, Venus, Copper or Brass, *Vishuddha chakra*; Pituitary, or post–nasal ganglion, Moon, Silver, *Ajna chakra*; Pineal gland, Mercury, Quicksilver, *Sahasrara chakra.* They are shown white, to indicate purification.

As said, one should beware of fixing attention upon the centers themselves. Their activity may be stimulated by engaging in the kinds of meditation suggested by the modes of intelligence attributed to the corresponding letters. Thus Saturn is represented in the Tarot by the World and Administrative Intelligence; Mars by the Tower and Exciting Intelligence; Jupiter by the Wheel of Fortune and Intelligence of Conciliation; the Sun by the card bearing the same name and Collective Intelligence; Venus by the Empress and Luminous Intelligence; the Moon by the High Priestess and Uniting Intelligence; Mercury by the Magician and Intelligence of Transparency.

Using the Tarot cards just enumerated as centers for concentration will arouse the activity of the corresponding centers without any danger of physical congestion. Remember, this is mental angling. This outline and its explanations are only guide posts. They are intended to tell you how to make use of the Tarot. They are not intended to make further investigation and study necessary. When Eliphas Levi promises the acquisition of a universal science from the Tarot, he implies that the student must use the cards for himself. I have just referred you to Patanjali's Yoga Aphorisms and its enumeration of the powers to be gained from meditation. The Tarot pictures are keys to the liberation of such powers by the same method. Behind their symbols are practical secrets of occultism which cannot be put into words. Lesser secrets, too, are hidden there, which might be written out; but my teachers have convinced me that such a course would be inadvisable. The plain truth is that the first rule in occult teaching is that the pupil should be told almost nothing that he can find out for himself. These lessons put you on the track of discovery. Your own work with the Tarot itself is the only thing that will bring you to the point where you will possess actual first-hand knowledge of the practical secrets of occultism.

The mountain in the background is to be understood as meaning what it does in the sixth and eighth trumps.

The bird on the bush is supposed to be a scarlet ibis. This is the Egyptian bird sacred to Hermes, the Magician. Its long bill is a natural fish-hook. Its correspondence to Mercury also alludes to the attribution of the direction South-Above to Tzaddi.

The woman is Hathor, or Mother Nature. In some respects we may identify her with the Empress. In others she corresponds to the High Priestess. For meditation is largely the utilization and direction of the powers of imagination and deduction peculiar to subconsciousness. But, it also depends upon subjective mind, because the knowledge gained in meditation is gleaned from the imperishable record of the memory of nature, symbolized by the scroll of the High Priestess.

Ten plants, growing near the edge of the pool, are symbols of the ten numerations, or aspects of the Life power's self-expression.

The pool is the universal consciousness, or reservoir of cosmic mind stuff, which is stirred into vibration by the act of meditation. This is indicated by the stream of water flowing into the pool from the right-hand pitcher. It indicates direct modification of the cosmic mind stuff, apart

150

from sensory experience. The stream flowing from the other pitcher divides into five streams, which flow back to the pool along the ground, and indicate the modifications of sensory experience in meditation.

One knee of the woman rests upon the earth. The other forms the angle of a square. Her right foot rests upon the pool. Thus the earth supports her weight, but she balances herself by water. That is, sensations derived from material forms are the main support of meditation, but these are balanced by experience gained direct from the subconscious.

This picture represents the third stage of spiritual unfoldment, the calm that follows the storm represented in the preceding picture. It is a period of quest and research. The light is dim, like starlight, but these stars are distant suns. Thus it is written: "When you have found the beginning of the way, the star of your soul will show its light."

THE MOON

Qoph (ק, Q, value 100) means *back of the head.* This is the part of the skull which contains the cerebellum and medulla oblongata. These parts of the brain belong to the animal part of human personality. The medulla, particularly, governs many of the most important vital functions. It never sleeps.

Head, moreover, means *chief* in Hebrew, as in English. In the sequence of the Hebrew alphabet, the letter Qoph, *back of the head,* precedes the letter Resh, which means *the head.* Thus Qoph is *back of the head* in the series of letters. It is therefore that which comes before the dominion and rulership of which the word *head* is a symbol. This is true, also, of the occult meanings of the letter Qoph, which relate to states of consciousness anterior to perfect control, and leading thereto.

Sleep is the function assigned to Qoph. It is the period of physiological repair, during which the cells of the body undergo subtle changes which make the advancing student of occultism ready to experience and understand facts concealed from ordinary men. These facts are the experiential basis of the Ageless Wisdom.

The word translated *sleep,* is from the Book of Formation. It is a technical term in Rabbinical Hebrew, spelled שינה, ShINH, and having the value 365. Furthermore, by transposition of letters it may be read חשׁין, HShIN, or Ha Shin, *the tooth*. Thus it is a word whose number, like the Greek abraxas, may be a mystery–term relating to the number of days and to the number of *eons* ruling the year. And it also hints at a correspondence to the *Holy Letter* Shin.

South–Below combines South (XIX, Sun) with Below (II, High Priestess). The suggestion is that the solar radiance is reflected by the subjective mind. That is, in the processes anterior to complete control, the directive action of cosmic tendencies is reflected into the personal sphere of action through the agency of subjective mental states. This is actually what happens. Up to a certain point, the cosmic Life power molds its vehicles without their cooperation, so to say, Later, those vehicles become aware of what is going on, and share consciously in the work.

Pisces, the Fishes, is a watery mutable sign. It is ruled by Jupiter (X, The Wheel of Fortune) and Neptune (XII, The Hanged Man). Consideration of the Tarot trumps here indicated will make the meaning clearer. The processes we are now learning about are the direct outcome of the *wheels within wheels* of the interlocking cycles and rotations of cosmic activities. At the same time, there is a point in human evolution, represented by the Hanged Man, at which we become aware of the fact that personality is really only a channel for the Great Work. This awareness is also part of the development process represented in the symbolism of the XVIIIth major trump. It is also related to the sign Pisces because that sign governs the feet of man, and because feet are the path makers, the sign relates to that Way whose beginning is found when meditation reveals the light of the *star of the soul.* Venus is said to be exalted in Pisces. That is to say, what the Empress symbolizes reaches its highest expression in this sign, and therefore in the process occultly corresponding to it. Thus we may expect to find that imagination plays an important part in the work now under consideration. The color corresponding to Pisces is violet–red. Its musical tone is B-natural.

Corporeal Intelligence means *body consciousness*, that is, the aggregate intelligence of the cells of the body. Curiously, the root of the word *corporeal* is a Hebrew verb which means *to rain upon*, and we shall find a hint of this in the symbolism of the Tarot trump.

The number XVIII is IX by reduction. The Hermit is the Goal of the path shown in this picture. With him we are united, according to occult teaching, whenever we experience dreamless sleep. For profound sleep is the state, according to Ageless Wisdom, in which personal consciousness is perfectly joined to the real I AM.

The Moon symbolizes the reflected light of the subjective mind. The drops of light falling from it on the path correspond to the implication that *corporeal* is related to *rain.* They are 15 Hebrew Yods, corresponding in number to the 15 ornaments on the Crown of the Hierophant and to the 15 petals of the rose on the banner of Death. They may also be taken to represent the three elementary and the twelve zodiacal letters of the alphabet.

The pool below is the same as that of the fourteenth and seventeenth trumps. It is the *great deep* of cosmic mind stuff out of which emerges the *dry land* of physical manifestation. From it all organic life proceeds.

The shellfish climbing from the pool is a symbol of the early stages of conscious unfoldment, wherein the individual seems to be isolated from the rest of nature.

The path, rising and falling, has been worn by the feet (Pisces) of those who have traveled this way before. It passes between two animals of the same genus, both canine. But the dog is a product of human adaptation, while the wolf remains as nature made him. Thus the path passes between the extremes of nature and art.

In the foreground it traverses cultivated ground, which symbolizes matters of more or less general knowledge; but eventually it comes to the towers which mark the boundaries of the known. Then it continues into the Beyond, whose blue distances represent the planes of consciousness open to us during sleep or trance. The path rises and falls, suggesting periodicity, wave motion, vibration. Yet it continually ascends, so that as one progresses, the time comes when his most depressed states of consciousness are at a higher level than some of his earlier exaltations.

This trump represents the fourth stage of spiritual unfoldment, wherein the knowledge gained by meditation is *incorporated* into the organism. It is the stage of organization, of bodybuilding in accordance with subconscious mental patterns. In the tableau of major trumps given at the beginning of this outline you will find the eighteenth trump at the bottom of a row of three cards. At the top is the Emperor, for Reason is the mental tool by which we prepare for right action. In the middle is Justice, representing the law of poised activity, because only by action may we make any progress. At the bottom is the Moon, symbolizing the actual organization of the body–cells. For without organism, there is neither function nor faculty. The unfoldment of our latent powers is made possible by physiological changes in these bodies of flesh and blood.

Thus it is written, "Flesh and blood cannot inherit the kingdom of God," because the changes we speak of now are not transmissible from generation to generation. Nature gives us the wild body. Art must perfect it. Yet a flesh and blood body is the necessary vehicle for mastery as expressed here on the physical plane, and though it cannot inherit the powers of adeptship, it can become the vehicle of those powers when rightly organized by adaptive methods.

THE SUN

Resh (ר, R, value 200) means the head and face of man. In the head are gathered together or collected all the distinctively human powers. The word *countenance*, in fact, is derived from a Latin verb meaning *to hold together, to contain.* Again the *head* of any project is its organizer, director, guiding power, manager, and its controller. Thus now we may expect to find in the Tarot symbols plain intimations of leadership and authority.

South is the place of the Sun's meridian height, the place of its greatest brilliance and power. It is the opposite of North (XVI, The Tower), and thus in the Tarot indicates the peace and calm which follows true enlightenment. The color is orange, the note D–natural.

The Sun is the heavenly body represented by Resh. We have found it exalted in Aries (IV, The Emperor) and ruling Leo (VIII, Strength). It is the power which reaches its highest manifestation in Reason, and which always and everywhere is the ruling force that makes effective the law symbolized by Strength.

Fruitfulness and Sterility is the pair of opposites ascribed to Resh. They are the extremes of expression in the manifestation of solar energy. The sun causes all growth, but it also makes deserts.

Collecting or Collective Intelligence is the

mode of consciousness. To collect is to assemble, bring together, combine, unify, embody, synthesize. The Collective Intelligence concentrates all the modes of consciousness that have gone before, and combines them together in a new form. Thus it is a regenerative mode of consciousness, incorporating all the elements of control in a new realization of personality.

As the number XIX may be reduced to X, while X in turn may be reduced to I, we are to understand that the symbolism of the picture now before us is logically dependent on that of the Magician (I) and on that of the Wheel of Fortune (X). It is also the final term of the series representing self–conscious intellection, namely I, IV, VII, X, XIII and XVI.

The title simply means the dominant symbol, which is a Sun with a human countenance. It represents the truth that the seemingly material forces of nature really are modes of a conscious energy essentially human in character and potencies. The rays of the Sun are alternately waved and straight. The wavy rays represent vibration. The straight ones represent radiation, which is apparently in straight lines.

Four sunflowers, representing the four Qabalistic *worlds*, turn, not toward the daystar, but toward the child, as if to hint that all creation turns to man for its final development.

The wall in the background also represents artistic development of natural conditions. It is, furthermore, a symbol of the Fence, hence of Cheth, and thus of Speech and all the ideas represented by the Chariot. Thus Life and the Word (flowers and wall) are in the background as modifying forces. But it is to be noted that the child rides away from the wall, as if he were leaving behind the conditions that it symbolizes. Thus Mr. Waite says, "It is the great and holy light which goes before the endless procession of humanity coming out from the walled garden of the sensitive life and passing on the journey home."

The child is fair, like the Fool, and like the Fool, wears a wreath and a red feather. The feather has the same meaning as that of the Fool. The wreath is of flowers, instead of leaves, intimating the near approach to the harvest of final realization and liberation.

The child is naked, in accordance with an old Qabalistic saying that Spirit clothes itself to come down, and divests itself of the garments of matter to go up. The nipples and navel of the child are the points of a water triangle, hinting at the letter Mem and the Hanged Man. For the stage of unfoldment represented by the Sun is the expression of the law the Hanged Man symbolizes.

His red banner signifies action and vibration. Its black staff is like the black wand of the Fool, but is tipped with a point, similar to the staff of the Charioteer, and like it, signifying concentration. The banner is carried in the left hand as an intimation that the measurement and control of vibration which it indicates has passed from self–consciousness (right hand) to subconciousness – has become automatic, in other words. Thus it is easy, and the great standard seems no burden to the boy.

He rides a horse, symbol of solar energy, similar to the horse of Death. He rides without saddle or bridle, because he represents perfect balance. That balance is maintained by his outstretched right hand, which represents self–consciousness. He is the regenerated personality, recognizing and affirming its unity with the Father, or Source of all. He leaves behind the artificial erections of race consciousness, and fares forth free and joyous on his journey home.

This is the fifth stage of unfoldment. It is a degree of adeptship, that of liberation from the limitations of physical matter and circumstances. It is also a grade of conscious self–identification with the One Life. Yet it is not final. For though it is a stage wherein all material forces are under the control of the adept, who, having himself become childlike, realizes in his own person the fulfillment of the promise *A little child shall lead them*; the person who has reached this grade still feels himself to be a separate, or at least distinct, entity. This is not full liberation, but it is a higher state than any of those preceding it. It is, in particular, the stage in which all the physical forces are dominated by the will of the adept, because he is the unobstructed vehicle of the One Will which always has ruled those forces, since the beginning.

JUDGMENT

Shin (ש, Sh, value 300) is pronounced *sheen*. It means *tooth*, probably a serpent's fang, and suggests sharpness, acidity, active manifestation. The number of the letter, 300, is the value of the Hebrew words *Ruach Elohim*, which mean *Life Breath of the Divine Ones*. We may understand this letter as a symbol of the power which tears down the limitations of form as teeth break up food. As the serpent's fang it represents a power which *kills* the false personality and its sense of separateness. (Observe that the corresponding Tarot card is placed below that named Death in the tableau given earlier.)

Fire is the element attributed to Shin. It is the particular quality of the solar force and of the Mars vibration. It is also the quality of the zodiacal signs represented by the Emperor, Strength and Temperance. Its color is scarlet, its musical tone C–natural.

Vulcan, a planet as yet unrecognized by exoteric astronomy but considered in the calculations of some astrologers, is also attributed to this letter.

Perpetual Intelligence is the mode of consciousness. Its name is derived from a Hebrew root meaning *to stretch*, implying that the Perpetual Intelligence is an extension beyond the limits of the modes of consciousness that we know. The name also implies everlastingness, eternity, and thus conscious immortality.

The number XX reduces to II. Thus we understand that the consciousness here represented is the culmination of mental activities originating in the cosmic memory (II, High Priestess). This picture is the last of a series including II, V, VII, XI, XIV and XVII.

The Judgment implies completion, decision, termination. It is the final state of personal consciousness, because that which is represented by the card of the Tarot following it is a state wherein personal consciousness is wholly obliterated in a higher realization.

Mr. Waite's version of the twentieth trump is less happy than any of his other departures from medieval symbolism. The three figures in the background have no real business there, and add nothing of importance to the real meaning of the design. The three in the foreground sufficiently convey the occult significance.

The Angel is the Divine Breath, or cosmic fire, yet he is obviously the angel Gabriel, not only because he carries a trumpet, but also because Gabriel is the angel of the element water, which is indicated by his blue robe. The action of heat upon water creates air, the substance of breath. That breath is specialized in sound, and the basis of sound is sevenfold. The seven basic tones are indicated by the lines radiating from the bell of the trumpet, itself an instrument of sound vibration. What these tones are, and how to employ them, is no material for discussion in this elementary treatise. Suffice to say that sound is the instrument of final liberation, and the seven tones are those which affect the seven interior stars by sympathetic vibration.

The banner on the cross should be exactly 5 by 5 units, so that the arms of the cross will include 9 out of the 25 square units on the face of the banner. 9 is the number of completion, and 5 is the number of adaptation. Complete adaptation is one, but only one, of the esoteric meanings of the banner.

The man, woman and child are shown with grayish flesh, to inform us that they are not seen on the physical plane of existence. Gray is the occult color associated with Wisdom; but here it refers particularly to the astral body, for this scene is in the astral plane.

There all things are reversed, hence the Man is now at the left of the picture, in a passive attitude, and the Woman on the right receives the influences of the angel in her outstretched hands. Note the correspondence of this stretching gesture to the basic meaning of the Hebrew word translated *Perpetual*. The child is the regenerated personality.

All three figures rise from rectangular coffins, which represent the three dimensions of the physical plane. Standing, so to say, at right angles to these coffins, they indicate the mathematical definition of the fourth dimension – that which is at right angles to the other three.

The coffins float upon a sea which is the final reservoir of those waters which begin in the robe of the High Priestess. Snowy mountains in the background indicate the heights of abstract thought, and suggest that what is here shown is derived from mathematical considerations.

The child's back is toward us, because he represents return to the Source of all. This card shows the sixth stage of unfoldment, in which personal consciousness is on the verge of blending with the universal. At this stage the adept realizes that his personal existence is nothing but the manifestation of the relation between self–consciousness and subconsciousness. He sees, too, that self–consciousness and subconsciousness are not themselves personal, but modes of universal consciousness. Thus he knows that in reality his personality has no separate existence. At this stage his intellectual conviction is confirmed by fourth dimensional experiences which finally blot out the delusion of separateness forever.

THE WORLD

Tau (ת, T, but sometimes Th, value 400) means signature or mark, but the mark is the cross. The Egyptian Tau is said to have been a tally for measuring the depth of the Nile, also a square for measuring right angles. Among the Hebrews it was a sign of salvation (Ezekiel ix. 4). Thus it is *a symbol of salvation from death, and of eternal life.* As representing a signature, this letter implies security, guaranty, pledge, and so on. A signature is what makes all business instruments valid. It therefore indicates the final seal and witness to the completion of the Great Work of liberation.

Center, sometimes called *the palace of holiness in the midst*, is the direction attributed to Tau. This palace of holiness is said to *sustain all things.* In Qabalistic writings it is said to be Jerusalem or Zion, where Man can commune with God. The Hebrew word for *palace* is היכל, HIKL, whose number, 65, is also the number of אדני, ADNI, Adonai, *Lord.* The center is that point which is the fifth dimension. In it all spatial relations are united in a single *here*, and all time relations in a single *now.* The realization of this one point is the culmination of concentration.

Saturn, according to mythology, ate his own children. He represents that which absorbs its own expressions back into itself. Saturn is exoterically the planet of inertia, concreteness, profundity, weight. It shares the rulership of Aquarius (XVIII, The Star) with Uranus, and is the ruler of Capricorn (XV, The Devil). It is also exalted in Libra (XI, Justice). Thus we have here a power which is active in meditation, which is the source of those apparent limitations which make us seek a way of escape from bondage, and which is expressed in the equilibrated action symbolized by Justice. Saturn's color is indigo, or blue violet. The musical note is A–natural.

Dominion and Slavery is the pair of opposites attributed to Tau. Right interpretation of the necessity for limitation in any form of manifested existence is the secret of dominion. Wrong interpretations of the same thing are the causes of our slavery to conditions. The clue to the right understanding is the aphorism, "He who would rule Nature must first obey her laws."

Administrative Intelligence is consciousness of participation in the cosmic government. It is entry into the kingdom of heaven as a fully enfranchised citizen, taking active part in the execution of its laws.

The number XXI is connected with XII and III. It is also the sum of the numbers from 0 to VI. Compare it with the cards mentioned. In particular, study it as the summation of the ideas represented by the cards from 0 to VI. Again, XXI is the culmination of the series of trumps numbered III, VI, IX, XII, XV and XVIII.

The World is the commoner title. Sometimes

this trump is named *The Universe* to indicate that the consciousness it represents is not merely terrestrial but truly cosmic.

The four animals at the corners of the design have been explained in connection with the tenth trump.

The ellipse surrounding the dancing figure is incorrectly drawn in this version. Its outline should be precisely of the proportions of the ellipse in the number diagram. It will then give a very close approximation to the quadrature of the circle, and will also be derived from the geometrical construction of the Hexagram, or figure of two interlaced triangles. On old Tarot cards – even on the exoteric 18th century designs – the true proportions are almost always given.

This ellipse is formed of four rows of leaves, representing the four *worlds*. In the present design they are quite obviously phallic symbols. The wreath itself, as an ellipse, is feminine. Thus the shape of the leaves and the shape of the ellipse suggest the combination of male and female, positive and negative, subject and object, conscious and subconscious. It is the interpenetration and blending of these two modes of consciousness which is characteristic in Cosmic Consciousness. The Two become One. Note, too, that the ellipse itself is the Zero sign, symbol in numbers of superconsciousness.

The horizontal 8–shaped bindings at the top and bottom of the wreath are those which were over the heads of the Magician and the Woman in Strength. They have the same meanings. But here they are read to suggest that the law symbolized in those pictures has been carried into action. The similarities between them, and their positions, suggest the Hermetic axiom, "That which is above is as that which is below."

The dancer represents the merging of self–consciousness with subconsciousness, and the blending of these two with superconsciousness. Occult tradition says that the scarf conceals the fact of male reproductive organs. In this highest of all conscious experience all sense of separate sex is lost, along with the blotting out of the sense of separate personality. The Dancer is the All–Father and the All–Mother, too. She is the Bride, but she is also the Bridegroom. She is the Kingdom and the King, (even as Kingdom in the Qabalah is called *Bride* and also named Adonai, *Lord.*)

She bears two wands, similar to those of the Magician. Sometimes they are represented as spirals – that in the right hand turning clockwise, the other counter–clockwise – to represent the spiral force of the Life power. The right hand wand symbolizes Involution, the other, Evolution.

This card signifies Cosmic Consciousness, or Nirvana. For descriptions of this state see Dr. Richard Maurice Bucke's *Cosmic Consciousness*, Ali Nomad's book of the same title, Ouspensky's *Tertium Organum*, Boehme's *Supersensual Life*, William James' *Varieties of Religious Experience*, and the writings of Swami Vivekananda.

170

The central fact of this experience is that he to whom it comes has firsthand knowledge that he is identical with the One Power which is, so to say, the Pivot and the Source of the whole cosmos. He knows also that through him the governing and directing power of the universe flows out into manifestation.

Words fail to give any adequate idea of this seventh stage of spiritual unfoldment. I shall leave it to your intuition to combine the suggestions of the picture with the meanings of the letter Tau. Here is a picture of what you really are, and of what the cosmos really is. The universe is the Dance of Life. The inmost, immortal, central Self of you –That is the Eternal Dancer.

N.B. Just a word about methods of study. For you must study the Tarot if you would acquire the universal science. Therefore:

Provide yourself with a looseleaf notebook, and set down therein all that comes to you when you study each separate card in detail.

Study carefully the tableau given in the first pages of this book.

Call up a picture, whenever you have a spare moment, and ponder its meaning.

Remember that every major trump is a pattern, a pictorial suggestion to your subconsciousness, which will reorganize your physical body as well as your ideas. We become like what we contemplate. Contemplate these pictures in spare moments, and they will alter your whole life in no long time.

TAROT DIVINATION

This method of divination is not intended for fortune telling. If you debase it to that purpose, you will cripple yourself spiritually. Its proper application is to the solution of serious questions, for yourself or others.

Before attempting to divine, learn the divinatory meanings of the 78 cards. Do not try divination until you have committed these meanings to memory, because the subconscious response and control of shuffling required for divination necessitate thorough knowledge of the meaning of every picture.

The divinatory meanings of the major trumps are:

O. The Fool. In spiritual matters: Originality, audacity, venturesome quest. In material affairs: Folly, eccentricity, inconsiderate action.

I. The Magician. Constructive power, initiative, skill, subtlety, craft, occult wisdom and power.

II. The High Priestess. All meanings derivable from duality. Fluctuation, reaction, secrets, things hidden, unrevealed future.

III.   The Empress. Fruitfulness, beauty, luxury, pleasure, success. Badly placed in a divinatory layout: Dissipation, luxuriousness, sensuality.

IV. The Emperor. Stability, power; reason; ambition; oversight; control.

V.   The Hierophant. Intuition, teaching, inspiration; marriage, alliance; occult force voluntarily invoked.

VI.   The Lovers. Attraction, beauty, love. Harmony of inner and outer life.

VII.   The Chariot. Triumph, victory, and the like.

VIII.   Strength. Action, courage, power, control of the life force.

IX. The Hermit. Wisdom from above, prudence, circumspection.

X.   The Wheel of Fortune. Destiny; good fortune; turn for the better.

XI. Justice. Strength and force, but arrested, as in the act of judgment. Legal affairs, lawsuits, when the question relates to material affairs.

XII.   The Hanged Man. In spiritual matters: Wisdom, surrender to the inevitable. In material affairs: Losses, reverses.

XIII. Death. Contrarieties; sudden change; death.

XIV. Temperance. Combination, adaptation, economy, management.

XV. The Devil. Bondage, materiality, necessity, force, fate.

XVI. The Tower. Danger, conflict, unforeseen catastrophes, ambition.

XVII. The Star. Insight; hope; influence over others.

XVIII. The Moon. Voluntary change; deception; hidden enemies.

XIX. The Sun. Liberation; gain; riches.

XX. Judgement. Decision, renewal; determines a matter.

XXI. The World. Synthesis; success; change of place.

DIVINATORY MEANING OF MINOR TRUMPS

SUIT OF WANDS

Ace	Energy, strength, enterprise; principle; beginning.
Two	Dominion.
Three	Established strength.
Four	Perfected work.
Five	Strife; competition.
Six	Victory after strife; gain.
Seven	Valor; courage in face of difficulties.
Eight	Activity; swiftness; approach to goal.
Nine	Preparedness; strength in reserve; victory after opposition.
Ten	Oppression; burden of ill–regulated power.
King	Dark man, friendly, ardent; honesty; possible inheritance.
Queen	Dark woman, magnetic, friendly. Business success.
Knight	Dark, friendly young man. Departure. Change of residence.
Page	Dark young man. Messenger. Brilliance, courage.

SUIT OF CUPS

Ace	Fertility, productiveness, beauty, pleasure.
Two	Reciprocity, reflection.
Three	Pleasure, liberality, fulfillment, happy issue.
Four	Contemplation. Dissatisfaction with material success.
Five	Loss in pleasure. Partial loss. Vain regret.
Six	Beginning of steady gain, but beginning only. New relations, new environment.
Seven	Illusionary success. Ideas, designs, resolutions.
Eight	Abandoned success; instability. Leaving material success for something higher.
Nine	Material success; physical well–being.
Ten	Lasting success; happiness to come.
King	Fair man; calm exterior. Subtle, violent, artistic.
Queen	Fair woman; imaginative, poetic. Gift of vision.
Knight	Fair man, Venusian, indolent. Arrival, approach.
Page	Fair, studious youth. Reflection. News.

SUIT OF SWORDS

Ace	Invoked force; conquest; activity.
Two	Balanced force; indecision; friendship.
Three	Sorrow, disappointment, tears. Delay, absence, separation.
Four	Rest from strife; relief from anxiety; Quietness, rest, rest after illness. NOT a card of death.
Five	Defeat, loss, failure, slander, dishonor.
Six	Success after anxiety; passage from difficulties; a journey by water.
Seven	Unstable effort; uncertainty; partial success.
Eight	Indecision; waste of energy in details; a crisis.
Nine	Worry; suffering, despair, misery. Loss.
Ten	Ruin, pain, desolation; sudden misfortune. NOT a card of sudden death. In spiritual matters: End of delusion.
King	Distrustful, suspicious man. Full of ideas, thoughts and designs. Care, observation, extreme caution.
Queen	Widowhood; mourning. A keen, quick, intensely perceptive, subtle woman. Usually fond of dancing.

SUIT OF SWORDS

Knight   Active, clever, subtle, skilful, domineering young man. Enmity, wrath, war.

Page   Vigilant, acute, subtle, active youth.

SUIT OF PENTACLES

Ace   Material gain, wealth, contentment.

Two   Harmony in midst of change.

Three   Construction; material increase; growth; financial gain.

Four   Earthly power; physical forces; skill in directing them.

Five   Concordance; affinity; adaptation. (Waite's symbolism shows that the concord and harmony are necessarily interior. The unfortunates out in the snow are the profane, those who have not grasped the inner light.)

Six   Material prosperity, philanthropy, presents.

Seven   Success unfulfilled; delay, but growth.

Eight   Skill in material affairs.

SUIT OF PENTACLES

Nine	Prudence; material gain; completion.
Ten	Wealth; riches; material prosperity.
King	Friendly, steady, reliable married man.
Queen	Generous, intelligent, charming, moody married woman.
Knight	Laborious, patient, dull young man.
Page	Diligent, careful, deliberate youth.

N.B. Pages may be young girls as well as young lads. Queens are not always married, but represent rather women with experience of life.

Before beginning to divine, be sure that the Querent (person for whom divination is made) has formulated his question. Explain to him that all questions come under four major heads – (a) work, business, and so forth; (b) love, marriage, or pleasure; (c) trouble, loss, scandal, quarrelling, and the like; (d) money, goods and such purely material matters. Be careful that the Querent does not tell you his question or its nature before you begin to divine.

Make your mind as passive as possible while

you are shuffling and laying out the cards. Do not try to guess. Go by what the cards suggest to you.

Do not limit yourself to the divinatory meanings given in the outline. They are general, and under the special circumstances of a divination, may be altered. Say what comes to you to say.

It is better to learn the meanings of the cards than to write the meanings on them. Better for yourself, and more impressive for the Querent. By learning the meanings of three cards a day, you may master the significance of the whole pack in 26 days.

In addition to the meanings given above, observe and learn the following additional points:

Kings and Queens usually show actual men and women connected with the matter.

Knights sometimes represent the coming or going of a matter, according to the direction in which they face.

Pages indicate young people, but often show opinions, thought, ideas – either in harmony with, or opposed to the subject.

A majority of:

WANDS – Energy, opposition, quarrel.

CUPS – Pleasure, merriment.

SWORDS – Trouble, sadness, sickness, death.

PENTACLES – Business, money, possessions.

MAJOR TRUMPS – Strong forces beyond the Querent's control.

COURT CARDS – Society, meetings of many persons.

ACES – Strength generally. Aces are always strong cards.

If a spread contains:

4 Aces – Great power and force.
3 Aces – Riches, success.
4 Knights – Swiftness, rapidity.
3 Knights – Unexpected meetings. Knights, as a rule, show news.
4 Queens – Authority and influence.
3 Queens – Powerful friends.
4 Kings – Meetings with the great.
3 Kings – Rank and honor.
4 Pages – New ideas or plans.
3 Pages – Society of the young.
4 Tens – Anxiety, responsibility.
3 Tens – Buying, selling, commerce.
4 Nines – Added responsibilities.
3 Nines – Correspondence.
4 Eights – Much news.
3 Eights – Much journeying.
4 Sevens – Disappointments.
3 Sevens – Compacts, contracts.
4 Sixes – Pleasure.
3 Sixes – Gain, success.
4 Fives – Order, regularity.

3 Fives – Quarrels, fights.
4 Fours – Rest, peace.
3 Fours – Industry.
4 Threes – Resolution, determination.
3 Threes – Deceit.
4 Twos – Conferences, conversations.
3 Twos – Reorganization, recommendation.

A card is strong or weak, well dignified or ill dignified according to the cards next it on either side. Cards of the same suit on either side strengthen it greatly for good or evil, according to their nature. Cards of opposite natures weaken it greatly, for either good or evil. Swords are inimical to Pentacles; Wands, inimical to Cups. Swords are friendly with Cups and Wands; Wands friendly with Swords and Pentacles.

If a card falls between two others which are inimical to each other, (as a Sword card between a Cup and a Wand), it is not much affected by either.

METHOD OF DIVINATION

The Significator – This is the card selected to represent the Querent.

Married Men – Kings.

Bachelors – Knights.

Women Past 18 – Queens.

Adolescents of Either Sex – Pages.

Some diviners use the Magician for men, the High Priestess for women. Others choose the major trump representing the sun sign of the Querent, on the hypothesis that the sun sign represents the true individuality of the person. In general, however, it is safer to choose one of the sixteen court cards, as indicated above. Choose the Significator according to your knowledge or judgment of the Querent's character, rather than according to his physical characteristics.

2. Shuffle the cards, until you feel like stopping.

3. Hand the cards to Querent, ask him to think of the question attentively, and cut the cards with his left hand. The Querent should restore the cut, that is, put the pile which was on the bottom before cutting above the pile consisting of the upper half of the pack.

4. Take the cards as cut, and place them on the table before you.

5. Cut the pack with the left hand, and place the top half to the left.

6. Cut each of these two packs to the left.

7. These four stacks represent I H V H from right to left.

8. Find the Significator. If in the I pack, the question refers to work, enterprise, ideas, and so forth; if in the H pack, to marriage, love, or pleasure; if in the V pack to trouble, loss, scandal, quarreling, and the like; if in the 2nd H pack, to money, goods, purely material matters.

9. Tell the Querent what he has come for. That is, from the position of the Significator in one of the 4 piles, declare to him the general nature of his question. If wrong, abandon the divination. Do not resume the attempt within two hours. Better, wait until another day.

10. If right, spread out the pack containing the Significator, arranging the cards in a circle or wheel.

11. Count the cards from the Significator, in the direction in which the figure printed on card faces. If the figure on the card faces neither right nor left, but straight out from the picture, count to your left.

N. B. It is advisable to arrange the cards on the table so that the Significator will be at the top of the wheel. But be careful not to alter the sequence of the cards in so doing.

The counting should invariably include the card from which you start. Thus, if the Significator is a Page, you will count Seven, and if the card the count ends with is a seven in one of the suits of minor trumps, you will begin your second count of seven with that card and so on. For Kings, Queens and Knights, count 4. For Pages, count 7. For Aces, count 11.

For small cards of minor trumps, count according to the number printed at the top.

For major trumps, count: 3 for elemental trumps, (O, FOOL; XII, HANGED MAN; XX,

JUDGMENT); 9 for the planetary trumps (those corresponding to double letters and pairs of opposites); 12 for trumps representing signs of the zodiac.

Make a story of these cards. It is the story of the beginning of the affair.

12. Pair the cards on either side of the Significator, then those outside them, and so on. Make another story, filling up details, omitted in the first.

These two stories may not be quite accurate, but it is to be remembered that your Querent does not, as a rule, know everything about the matter. Nevertheless, the main outlines should be such as he can recognize. If not, abandon the operation at this point.

SECOND OPERATION

Develops the question.

1. Shuffle and let Querent cut, as before.

2. Deal the cards into 12 packs, for the 12 astrological houses of heaven.

3. Find the Significator. According to house in which it is found, judge that the matter will be affected by the general quality of that house.

The meanings of the houses are:

First – The person himself.

Second – His finances. Gain or loss, according to the cards found in this pile.

Third – Brothers, sisters. Short journeys, writings, mental inclinations and abilities.

Fourth – Father, home, environment, domestic affairs, lands, mines and real estate generally.

Fifth – Children, love affairs, pleasure, speculation.

Sixth – Sickness, servants, employers, food, clothing, hygiene, service, small animals.

Seventh – Unions, partnership, marriage, contracts, dealings with others, and the public generally, legal affairs, open enmities.

Eighth – Death, psychic experiences of the spiritistic kind, all matters connected with the dead, such as legacies, etc. Also financial affairs of the business or marriage partner.

Ninth – Long journeys, foreign countries, places remote from birthplace, philosophy, religion, education, dreams, visions, psychic development.

187

Tenth – Profession, occupation, honor, fame, promotion, mother, employer. Also government affairs.

Eleventh – Friends, associations, hopes and fears.

Twelfth – Unseen or unexpected troubles, hidden or secret enmities. Restraint, limitations, hospitals, prisons, insane asylums, sanitariums, and the like. Secret societies, occultism of the practical sort, and organizations devoted to it. Large animals.

4. Spread out the pile containing the Significator, as in former operation, and count and pair as before. Remember that the two stories thus developed must be more or less colored by the nature of the house in which the Significator falls.

THIRD OPERATION

1. Shuffle, and let the Querent cut, as before.

2. Deal cards into twelve stacks, representing the signs of the zodiac.
   Even if you have no astrological information particularly, you can judge the general meaning of the signs, because each is represented by a major trump. For example, if the Significator should fall in the stack corresponding to Cap-

ricorn, the further development of the question would be in accordance with the occult meaning of the letter Ayin and the 15th major trump. If a material question, it would probably denote limitation. If one of pleasure, danger or over–indulgence on the sense side. Your own knowledge of the trumps will help you in this.

The order of the 12 signs is:

Aries	IV	Emperor
Taurus	V	Hierophant
Gemini	VI	Lovers
Cancer	VII	Chariot
Leo	VIII	Strength
Virgo	IX	Hermit
Libra	XI	Justice
Scorpio	XIII	Death
Sagittarius	XIV	Temperance
Capricorn	XV	Devil
Aquarius	XVII	Star
Pisces	XVIII	Moon

3. Find Significator, count and pair as before.

FOURTH OPERATION

1. Shuffle, and let the Querent cut, as before.

2. Deal cards into ten stacks. Each stack corresponds to one of the Sephiroth, and thus to one of the statements of being in the B. O. T. A. affirmations. Thus, if the Significator should fall in the seventh pile, the conclusion of the divination would all be colored by the statement *Living from that Will, supported by its unfailing Wisdom and Understanding, mine is the Victorious life,* and your advice to the Querent would all proceed from that basic idea.

3. Find Significator, count and pair as before.

As a rule, but not always, the first operation shows past time, particularly in the pairing of cards, when those which are in the pile away from which the Significator faces will usually indicate past time. If he faces out, those on your right will be past time as a rule.

Experience alone will enable you to judge time with any degree of accuracy, and no rules can be given. If you are possessed of the psychic qualifications necessary to a diviner, you will *feel* time.

Finally, let me reiterate the thought that this is not to be used for vulgar fortune telling, or to amuse a party of friends. If you yield to the temptation so to abuse this information, you will pay for it in the loss of all power of true divination, and probably in the loss of ability to control the higher rates of psychic vibration. Thus the ultimate result of abuse of this divinatory practice will be to make you more negative, more the slave of circumstance, more liable to evil of every kind.

For further information on astrology, consult The New A to Z Horoscope Maker and Delineator (Revised and Expanded), by Llewellyn George, published by the Llewellyn Publishing Co. It contains everything one needs to know.

For further information about the Tarot, the work of the Builders of the Adytum, and so on, contact B.O.T.A. at

5101 North Figueroa Street
Los Angeles, CA 90042
Phone: (323) 255-7141 – Fax (323) 255-4166
Email: inquiries@bota.org